POSITIONED TO WIN

THE ESSENCE OF EPHESIANS

JACK AIKEN

Published in Beaverton, Oregon, by Good Book Publishing.
www.goodbookpublishing.com
V1.1

Printed in the United States of America

TABLE OF CONTENTS

PREFACE

One has to wonder why someone, such as this author, with no formal academic background in biblical studies, would have the audacity to attempt to write an in-depth study on the Book of Ephesians. The simple answer is that as we have attempted to prepare ministers for the various credential levels in the Assemblies of God, we have not been able to find a textbook that was written from a Pentecostal and an Arminian doctrinal position. So I decided to do it myself.

The Book of Ephesians contains several passages that address core issues of Pentecostal doctrine. Commentators and authors who do not come from a Pentecostal background often interpret these passages in ways that require the Pentecostal instructor to refute the author's position. This may not always have a negative result, but the potential for confusion in the mind of the student is magnified.

The Book of Ephesians also contains a number of passages which take on significantly different meanings, depending on the commentator's position on the Arminian-Calvinist doctrinal spectrum. While not every Assemblies of God minister is a strict Arminian, neither are there many who are "five-point-Calvinists."

Not all of us in the Assemblies of God know what to do with those Scriptures that allow for a predestinarianism interpretation, but almost all of us believe that human free will is a factor in one's becoming a Christian and in their being successful as a lifelong follower of Christ.

While some of the material in the following pages is the product of my own independent thinking, for the most part, it is a consolidation and condensation of materials accumulated in my brain during 24 years of teaching and preaching ministry.

My desire is to produce a study of the Epistle to the Ephesians that is devotional and conversational and viewed through an Arminian-Holiness-Pentecostal lens.

CHAPTER 1
INTRODUCTION

The Epistle of Paul to the Ephesians is one of the most significant pieces of biblical literature. In its impact on Christian theology, it may be unsurpassed. Ephesians is a timeless book, and it could well have been written to the modern 21st Century church. It describes human beings, who, even with increasing education levels, advancing technology and changing cultures, remain, in all the essentials, unchanged.

We are still sinful; we are still subject to the deceptions of the evil one. We still have no ability to save ourselves from the problems of our world, let alone save ourselves spiritually. However, Ephesians does not leave us without hope. It describes a God Who has reached out to mankind to redeem, restore and transform each person in such a way as to create a whole new society bound together in Christ.

The message of Ephesians is about a loving God Who is actively drawing men to Himself. It is about the reality of Christians being one with Christ, being in Him and having the ability to live different lives as a result of that intimate relationship.

Ephesians actually presents us with the expectation, or rather the requirement, that the union with Christ is to be reflected in the lives we live.

Through the spirit - not our efford"

Ephesians draws a distinct line between the life before Christ and the life after Christ. "For you were once darkness, but now you are light in the Lord. Live as children of light" (Ephesians 8:8). This is intended to bring people to understand that they are not to live like the society in which they are immersed, but to display their life in Christ in practical, observable ways.

However, Ephesians, for all its emphasis on holy living, does not take a legalistic approach. It does not give a list of "dos" and "don'ts" or even a series of rules to follow, yet the letter points to the necessity of a radical change of the inner being coupled with a lifestyle which reflects the change. However, Paul always points to the Holy Spirit as the source of that change, not our own efforts. In essence, we have no internal ability to change ourselves, but Paul makes sure we are aware of our ability to impede the Holy Spirit's efforts to change us.

Ephesians is intensely relational. All relationships are viewed from the perspective of our relationship with Christ. We are "in Christ" and are part of His body, made up of all believers. A properly functioning body requires its individual members to be at peace and in unity.

Ephesians does not discuss worship or prayer directly, but the letter contains several sections that are, in fact, prayers and expressions of praise.

The first chapter consists exclusively of praises and prayers. Paul may have actually been quoting from liturgical prayers and hymns that were in current use in the early church.

Chapter 1

In our study of the Letter to the Ephesians, we are going to look at a section primarily from a devotional perspective, although, occasionally, we will take a more technical look at some passages.

Chapter 2
The Ephesian Context

To Whom Was the Letter Written?

Anytime you pick up a letter from your mailbox, the first thing you want to know is from whom the correspondence has come. However, to the messenger, the thing that is of greatest importance is to whom the correspondence is addressed. In the first verse of the Book of Ephesians, these two questions appear to be adequately answered. Paul the Apostle identifies himself as the author and sender of the letter, and he addresses the "saints which are at Ephesus." So why can we not take this information at face value and leave it at that? We certainly can, and perhaps we should, without question, but as we study the Letter to the Ephesians today, we must realize we are almost 2,000 years removed from the culture in which it was written. Additional knowledge of the culture from non-biblical sources is constantly emerging, and these discoveries can open our eyes to cultural realities and may serve to broaden or sharpen our understanding of biblical materials without casting doubt on their essential accuracy.

For example, we understand that in that time it was not unusual for a letter to be addressed in such a way as to indicate that while the interested parties at a certain location were to be the first to receive the correspondence, it was to be circulated to all other interested parties in the surrounding area. Such a letter was called an encyclical letter. We can find evidence of this practice in the early church in the letter to the Colossians. In verse 4:16, we read, "And when this epistle is read among you, cause it to be read also in the church of Laodicea; and that you likewise read the epistle from Laodicea." It is quite possible that this letter to the Ephesians was such a letter.

There are also several features of the letter itself that would support such a conclusion. First, a major theme of the letter is unity in Christ between all believers. This is a general theme applicable to Jew or Gentile, regardless of their geographical location. Second, it addresses no specific problem as do so many of Paul's other letters. Third, it contains no greetings to specific individuals, which is also a rather consistent part of Paul's correspondence.

Since letters of that day consisted of tightly rolled and sealed scrolls, carried by messenger, there would be no record of what specific directions the messenger may have received from the sender about the circulation of the communication. It is possible that while the letter is addressed internally to the saints at Ephesus, the verbal instructions accompanying the scroll may have delineated a wider distribution.

This question is interesting but is in no way critical to our understanding of the message the Letter to the Ephesians brings to us 21st Century Christians.

The History of the Ephesian Church

The story of the Ephesian church starts with Paul's second missionary journey which began sometime in 49 A.D. and extended into 52 A.D. As this trip was being planned, Paul had a heated debate with Barnabas, his companion on the first missionary excursion. Barnabas wanted to include John Mark in the party, but Paul strenuously objected because Mark had begun but not completed the first missionary trip, and this failure, in Paul's mind, disqualified him for further ministry, at least with him.

This dispute led to a parting of the ways between Paul and Barnabas. Barnabas took Mark and embarked on a missionary journey of his own. Paul then selected Silas and began his second missionary journey as recorded in the Book of Acts. Launching from Jerusalem, they went north to Antioch (Syria) and then on to Derbe and Lystra, where Timothy joined them for the rest of the trip.

After completing a circuit through Macedonia, Ephesus was their last stop in Asia as they made their way back to Jerusalem. Aquila and Priscilla, who were traveling with Paul at this time, were left in Ephesus, presumably to begin preaching the gospel there. Paul proceeded on to Caesarea, then to Jerusalem and finally back to Antioch, where he spent some time before beginning his third missionary journey.

This third trip took Paul through Derbe, Iconium and Antioch in Galatia before he arrived at Ephesus. Here Paul and his party met a group of 12 believers, who had come

CHAPTER 2

to believe in Jesus through the ministry of Apollos. Apollos was a powerful preacher and taught accurately about Jesus and the plan of salvation, despite the fact that he knew only the baptism of John the Baptist, which was a baptism for repentance. After hearing Apollos preach in the synagogue at Ephesus, Aquila and Priscilla took him aside and explained to him the gospel more fully. Just what this additional teaching consisted of is not known. Apparently, Apollos left Ephesus shortly after his encounter with Aquila and Priscilla, going on to Achaia and then to Corinth.

While Apollos was in Corinth, Paul arrived in Ephesus, and something in his conversations with the believers there led him to ask them, "Did you receive the Holy Spirit when you believed?" Their answer revealed that they had not even heard of the Holy Spirit. Consequently, Paul baptized them in water in the name of Jesus and then laid hands on them and prayed for them that they would be baptized in the Holy Spirit. Immediately, they received the Holy Spirit in much the same way as the disciples had received Him on the Day of Pentecost, meaning that their Spirit baptism was accompanied by speaking in tongues and prophesying.

From the Pentecostal perspective, this incident lends strong support for the belief that the baptism in the Holy Spirit is a distinct and separate experience from conversion and is subsequent to it.

Paul never called their salvation through faith in Jesus Christ into question, but baptized them in the name of

[handwritten margin note: Not faithwe's in these only Baptism in Holy Spirit?]

Jesus and then prayed for them to receive the Holy Spirit. The receiving of Holy Spirit baptism subsequent to the salvation experience can also be seen or strongly inferred in the case of the original disciples on the Day of Pentecost, in the case of the Samaritan believers, in the experience of the Gentiles at Cornelius' house and in Paul's own conversion and subsequent Spirit baptism in Damascus. All of these experiences are detailed in the Book of Acts.

After three months of trying to minister to the Jews in the synagogue, Paul withdrew from the synagogue and spent the next two years teaching daily in the school of Tyrannus.

During these two years, the Lord worked many mighty miracles through Paul. It was in Ephesus where the seven sons of Sceva attempted to cast out demons in the name of Jesus. It was in Ephesus where the new believers brought their books of magic to be burned. The value of these books was 50,000 pieces of silver, which probably refers to the Greek drachma, roughly equivalent to a day's wage for an ordinary working man. At today's minimum wage of about $65 per day, the value in today's economy would be about 3.25 million dollars.

It was also during this time that the gospel began to have such an impact on the sales of souvenir silver likenesses of the Goddess Diana (Artemis) that the local craftsmen, fearing for their livelihood and for the honor of their goddess, stirred up a great riot against Paul and the local believers. In the wake of this rioting, Paul called the

18

Chapter 2

brethren together, embraced them and left Ephesus to return to the churches in Macedonia.

Paul's last personal contact with the Ephesians occurred toward the end of the third missionary journey as he was making his way back to Jerusalem. When he arrived at Miletus, he sent for the Ephesian elders, told them of the prophecies of his coming imprisonment and blessed them. They wept as he departed because of his word to them that they would see his face no more.

As the Spirit had foretold, Paul was bound and imprisoned and eventually transported to Rome to await trial before Caesar. It was during this period of house arrest, chained to a Roman guard, that Paul wrote the Letter to the Ephesians.

Questions About Paul's Authorship

The text (1:1) of the Epistle to the Ephesians identifies the Apostle Paul as the writer. The text (3:1) also states that Paul was a prisoner at the time of the writing. There seems to be no concrete reason to doubt the authenticity of the internal statements, however, some scholars contest the authorship of Paul on the basis that there are words used in this letter that are not used by Paul in his other writings. They also point to the fact that the wording, sentence structure and doctrinal statements are also somewhat different. Some critics suggest that the language in the Letter to the Ephesians is more sophisticated than that in the writings commonly agreed to have been authored by Paul.

was he?

None of these objections mandate an authorship other than Paul. Paul was a brilliant man and as such should have been well able to vary his language and style as he addressed different subject matter and different audiences. Furthermore, there are many more similarities between this letter and Paul's other letters than there are differences. In fact, many verses in Ephesians are identical to those in other letters. For example, there are 55 verses in the Epistle to the Ephesians that are also found in the Epistle to the Colossians.

The Date of Writing

We know from the internal evidence of the text itself that Paul was in prison at the time he wrote the Epistle to the Ephesians. Tradition has it that Paul suffered two imprisonments in Rome. The first we read about in the Book of Acts, and this imprisonment was probably between the years 60 to 62 A.D. It seems likely that he was released from this captivity and continued his missionary travels, perhaps achieving his goal of going to Gaul or the areas we know as Spain and France today. There is a tradition from England that Paul may have even reached its shores during this time of freedom.

The record of his ministry after his first imprisonment and the circumstances of his second arrest are shrouded in mystery, but would have probably occurred during the persecution that arose during the reign of the Emperor Nero. It is fairly certain that Paul was executed in Rome by decapitation around 65 A.D. after a stay in the Mamertine

CHAPTER 2

prison. During this second imprisonment, he wrote other letters in which he writes of his impending death, which would seem inconsistent with the lenient imprisonment he suffered in Rome after his transfer from Caesarea Maritima.

Scholars who doubt the Pauline authorship of this epistle date its writing to a time between 70 and 170 A.D.

Cultural Atmosphere of Ephesus

Archeological excavations on the West Coast of Asia Minor indicate that Ephesus was already settled as long as 8,000 years ago, somewhere around 6000 B.C. Although the fortunes of Ephesus declined over the centuries as its harbor silted up, it continued as a place of significant habitation until it was completely abandoned in the 15th Century.

Ephesus was the chief commercial city of the region and probably the second largest city in the Roman Empire at the time Paul lived and ministered there. William Barclay, in his commentary, The Revelation of John (Vol. 1, p.58), made the following comments about Ephesus: "Ephesus was the Gateway of Asia (Minor). One of its distinctions, laid down by statute, was that when the Roman proconsul came to take up office as governor of Asia, he must disembark at Ephesus and enter his province there. For all the travelers and the trade, from the Cayster and the Maeander Valleys, from Galatia, from the Euphrates and from Mesopotamia, Ephesus was the highway to Rome. In later times, when Christians were brought from Asia to be flung to the lions in the arena in Rome, Ignatius called Ephesus the Highway of the Martyrs."

People of all nations to the west and to the east were constantly passing through its streets and making their imprint on the composite culture. Tremendous business was generated by the meeting of the needs and desires of these travelers. This traffic was multiplied because Ephesus was famous for its Temple of Artemis, the Greco-Roman goddess also known as Diana. This world-famous temple was first completed about 550 B.C., and although it had been destroyed and rebuilt, it continued as a pagan worship shrine until it was destroyed one final time by a Christian mob in 401 A.D.

The worship of Artemis involved all sorts of activities that both Jews and Christians would have considered wickedness and violations of the moral law of God. Ephesus was a city rife with superstition, and magic arts were practiced by much of the population. We see evidence of this in Acts 19:19-20: "And many who had believed came confessing and telling their deeds. Also, many of those who had practiced magic brought their books together and burned them in the sight of all. And they counted up the value of them, and it totaled fifty thousand pieces of silver. So the word of the Lord grew mightily and prevailed" (NKJV).

Artemis was the goddess of fertility, and ritual prostitution was a common practice associated with her worship.

Chapter 2

Ephesus would not appear to be a place friendly to the gospel, with its atmosphere of superstition, magic arts and open sexual promiscuity. However, Paul's preaching of the gospel had such impact as to bring about violent persecution as a result of the economic ramifications resulting from the conversion of large numbers of Ephesians. It is significant to note that there is no mention of the apostles directing any picketing or demonstrations against the Temple of Artemis. They just preached the gospel with the anointing and with demonstrations of power, and the result was so many conversions that the sale of images of Artemis went into a steep decline.

The Scriptures certainly assure us that Jesus is the same yesterday, today and forever, and the preaching of His gospel is still perfectly capable of the same dramatic results. Since Jesus has not changed, and the power of the gospel has not changed, it behooves us to ask ourselves just what has changed since very few churches or ministries of our day are having this kind of economic impact on the sin-based industries of our time.

Major Theme and Broad Outline

The overriding theme of the letter to the Ephesians is unity among believers. In Christ, both Jew and Gentile are united by faith into one new people of God, the church. Christ is the Head of the church and His body consists of all believers, regardless of race, ethnicity or former belief system.

A broad outline of the Letter to the Ephesians,

consisting of three words, "Sit, Walk, Stand," has been expounded upon by Watchman Nee. Our discussion will follow that same general path.

Where we "Sit" with Christ is outlined in Chapters 1-3. This is a doctrinal section which speaks of the believer's position in Christ: "God made us sit together in the heavenly places in Christ" (Ephesians 2:6). This position in Christ includes spiritual blessings, forgiveness of sin, blamelessness, power, redemption, adoption, security and acceptance.

The Christian "Walk" is described in Chapters 4-6 and comprises a practical section addressing how the believer is to behave based on the position he has been granted in Christ. The emphasis is on the necessary elements that mark the lifestyle of the disciple and committed follower of Christ.

The Christian's ability to "Stand" is addressed in chapter 6, verses 10 through 18, where Paul describes the "whole armor of God." Properly understood, the armor of God is a reminder that Christ is our defender and is a metaphor for all the ways in which Christ enables us to stand against the onslaughts of the evil one. This section brings us full circle back to our position in Christ, which mandates our behavior and provides unfailing protection against the enemy of our souls.

In summary, the Ephesians' letter focuses on the fact that we all are made one in Christ, and being in Christ, we should therefore live our lives so that they reflect His nature and character. Specifically, Paul emphasizes God's plan for the salvation of all believers, both Jew and Gentile, through the death and resurrection of His Son, Jesus Christ.

CHAPTER 3
IN CHRIST

Ephesians 1:1-4:

Paul, an apostle of Jesus Christ by the will of God, to the saints which are at Ephesus, and to the faithful in Christ Jesus: ²Grace be to you, and peace, from God our Father, and from the Lord Jesus Christ. ³Blessed be the God and Father of our Lord Jesus Christ, who hath blessed us with all spiritual blessings in heavenly places in Christ: ⁴According as he hath chosen us in him before the foundation of the world, that we should be holy and without blame before him in love: (KJV).

Saints By the Grace of God

An ever-present theme in the Letter to the Ephesians is the glory of God revealed in the church of Jesus Christ, which God has predestined to be "a glorious church, without spot or wrinkle or any such thing, but that she should be holy and without blemish." If the corporate body of Christ is to appear in this glorious state, then it stands to reason that those members who make up this body will also be, in some mysterious and spiritual way, "without spot or wrinkle, or any such thing" (Ephesians 5:27).

In reality, however, when we look at ourselves and other members of the body of Christ, we see anything but that spotless, wrinkle-free ideal. Eventually, we must come to realize that neither we, nor our fellow believers, are capable of raising ourselves to this higher standard. This tendency to focus on our weaknesses leads us to a crisis of confidence in Christ's ability to elevate us to this higher plane of perfection. However, Christ has committed Himself to the production of this perfected church, and according to Romans 8:29, God has predestined every believer to be conformed to the image of His Son.

[handwritten marginal note: Arminian ?]

The Blessings of Being in Christ (Ephesians 1:5-8)

"Having predestinated us unto the adoption of children by Jesus Christ to himself, according to the good pleasure of his will, [6]To the praise of the glory of his grace, wherein he hath made us accepted in the beloved. [7]In whom we have redemption through his blood, the forgiveness of sins, according to the riches of his grace; [8]Wherein he hath abounded toward us in all wisdom and prudence;" (KJV).

Ephesians 1:1-8 delineates our starting position in Christ. Everyone who is in Christ by faith has already come into "every spiritual blessing in the heavenly places in Christ." As Paul describes our spiritual position as believers, he uses this phrase, "in Christ," or some variation of it, over and over. He describes the blessings that accrue to us merely by virtue of the fact that the Holy Spirit has baptized us into the body of Christ. These blessing are ours immediately upon our entry into Him by faith.

[handwritten note at bottom: Paul's "in Christ" is different now than how I've been using it]

The word "blessed" means to be in highly favorable circumstances. Some have defined it as "happy, to be envied." Jesus used the word "blessed" repeatedly in the Beatitudes (Matthew 5:3-10).

In verses 4-8, Paul lists a series of highly favorable circumstances in which every true believer, or rather obedient follower of Christ, finds himself. These favorable circumstances include being chosen, adopted, accepted and redeemed in Christ.

Chosen

First, we find we are "chosen in Christ." Those from a Calvinist theological perspective will see in this support for the idea that some people are predestined by God to be saved, while others are predestined to be lost. Others, from an Arminian position, will argue that to be chosen in Christ refers only to the means by which sinners are brought into a right relationship with God. In other words, God has chosen to bring sinners to Himself through faith in Christ and His substitutionary sacrifice on the cross.

For those who have come into Christ by faith, this Calvinist/Arminian debate becomes moot. We are chosen; we are saved by grace through faith, and we are in Christ. We are chosen, and we can rejoice in the certainty of our election. Jesus said in John 15:16, "You did not choose Me, but I have chosen you and appointed you that you should go and bear fruit …"

We are predestined to be saved through the hearing of

the gospel. No one will be saved who has not heard the gospel. So whether or not God has predestined some to be saved and some to be lost, the Great Commission remains the same: "Go into all the world and preach the gospel to every creature" (Mark 16:15).

While the Bible clearly states that "whosoever will" may come to Christ, this does not deny that God, Who is all-knowing, knows "from the foundation of the world" who will accept His gracious invitation. Without appearing to be disingenuous, we can conclude that every individual freely chooses to do what God in His foreknowledge knows they will do. Because of this foreknowledge, God can use the Pharaohs and Judases of the world to further His purposes without being accused of unfairness, because their choices, while foreknown, were not foreordained. In other words, God has always known where our free will will take us.

Therefore, where we spend eternity will be based on our freely chosen action, not on an arbitrary (at least in our understanding) decision by God. Anyone who is lost will be lost because of his choosing to sin. Anyone who enters into eternal life will do so because he has believed in Jesus as his personal Savior and has given his life over to following Him.

Adopted

Not only are we chosen in Christ, but we have also been adopted. We have been given the place of a son, and not just any son, but the firstborn son who is destined to receive his Father's wealth and estate.

We do not enter the family of God as a servant, but as an heir to all the Father possesses. Paul wrote to the Romans that we are "heirs of God and joint heirs with Christ" (Romans 8:17), and he emphasizes this fact again in his Letter to the Galatians. Every believer is "an heir of God through Christ" (Galatians 4:7).

God has given all things into the hands of His Son, and His Son has chosen us to be "in Him," and in Him we share His inheritance.

In the natural world, multiple heirs only benefit from the portion of the estate allocated to them; however, in the spiritual realm, every heir is the equivalent of a sole heir of God. We all get it all, because in Christ we are all firstborn sons of the Father.

Accepted

In addition to being selected and adopted as firstborn sons, we are also accepted. Accepted doesn't mean to be barely tolerated, it means "endued with special honor." It carries the connotation of being "highly favored." God by His grace — by His own design and work on our behalf — has bestowed upon every believer a measure of the special honor and great favor He also bestows on His only begotten Son.

Redeemed

Redeemed = Redemption

Paul lists redemption as the fourth great benefit we receive "in Christ." We are redeemed by the blood of

Christ. The "blood" is a metaphor for Christ's death as a substitutionary sacrifice for our sins. To redeem means to "buy back." A prisoner of war or a kidnap victim could be said to be redeemed or bought back. Redeemed means to be returned to your former state through the full payment of the ransom demanded by your captors.

The concept of redemption can be understood in another way. In the days of the Roman Empire, a person could sell himself into slavery in order to provide a means of survival, or one could be forced into slavery because of a debt that he could not pay. In time, should he prosper economically in his servitude, he might eventually be able to buy his own freedom or redeem himself. And it was possible, though not likely, that some benefactor might buy his freedom for him.

In a real sense, all humanity finds itself held captive by sin, but it is God, not Satan, who has set the price for release from the slavery of sin. Every human being since Adam and Eve has been born physically alive, but spiritually dead. Being spiritually dead, they are separated from God and have no relationship with Him. Therefore, we can say human beings are born into spiritual slavery; if they are not released from their spiritual slavery by being born again during the span of their physical lives, they will enter eternity spiritually dead and will continue to be separated from God and His love. This is the "second death."

Through the death of Christ, or by the shedding of His blood, God has provided our redemption price or ransom.

When this redemption price is appropriated by faith in Christ, He provides complete freedom from the slavery of sin. The power of sin is broken in our lives, and sin no longer has any dominion over us.

At the moment we receive Jesus as Savior, we are no longer bound to sin. True, all Christians continue to sin after they have been redeemed. However, the incidents of sinful behavior should decrease rapidly in intensity and frequency as the Holy Spirit, in the process of sanctification, conforms each one to the image of Christ.

Sanctified

Sanctification is both instantaneous and progressive. When we accept Christ as Savior and are justified by faith, we become as holy in God's sight as we will ever be, because the blood of His Son has completely covered our sin. This is instantaneous sanctification.

Progressive sanctification refers to the process of the development of the image of Christ in the individual believer, which will be observed by others as he continually changes toward more Christ-like attitudes and behaviors.

Christ's blood is not an installment payment on redemption, nor is it a down payment or something to be delivered in the future upon further payments. Jesus' blood has bought your freedom from sin and slavery to the devil. If you are redeemed, you are free; no additional payment is necessary; no additional work must be done.

While many Christians are not experiencing their full

redemption, it is not because of some limitation of what Jesus has done. He has set us completely free. Christians don't need exorcism, they just need to reckon daily on the power of God and be brought into full understanding of what Jesus has already accomplished for them. He has given us total liberty from sin's dominion, not some sort of parole or conditional release, but a pardon, full and free. The pardon from sin Jesus gives means the consequences of the offense are totally rescinded and, furthermore, can never be reinstated.

CHAPTER 4
THE MYSTERY

Ephesians 1:9-14:

Having made known unto us the mystery of his will, according to his good pleasure which he hath purposed in himself: [10] That in the dispensation of the fullness of times he might gather together in one all things in Christ, both which are in heaven, and which are on earth; even in him: [11] In whom also we have obtained an inheritance, being predestinated according to the purpose of him who worketh all things after the counsel of his own will: [12] That we should be to the praise of his glory, who first trusted in Christ. [13] In whom ye also trusted, after that ye heard the word of truth, the gospel of your salvation: in whom also after that ye believed, ye were sealed with that Holy Spirit of promise, [14] Which is the earnest of our inheritance until the redemption of the purchased possession, unto the praise of his glory (KJV).

The Mystery Revealed in Christ

Four words demand our attention in this passage: mystery, inheritance, sealed and guarantee. In the murder mystery literature of today, you begin with a circumstance whose explanation is hidden.

As the story unfolds, the detective, often at great personal risk, will begin to investigate and slowly uncover the chain of events that led up to the present tragedy. A good mystery story will not only reveal the "whodunit," but the motive and the method. Frequently the future prospects of those who had recently been under suspicion will be laid out, revealing a "happy ever after" ending for the innocent.

The mystery to which Paul refers is somewhat different. We already know "whodunit." Death came to all mankind through the sin of Adam. The mystery is, "How will God negate the effects of sin and reconcile the world to Himself?"

To further complicate matters, for many centuries the world did not know that God had any intention of making a provision by which sins could be forgiven. Even God's chosen people had no understanding that God's redemptive plan would be extended not only to them, but to Gentiles as well.

In Christ, the mystery was revealed.

In Christ, God's intention to reconcile the entire world to Himself was revealed.

In Christ, the means by which this redemption would be accomplished is revealed.

In Christ, the future of humanity is revealed. John 3:16 spells it out clearly. "For God so loved the world that He gave His only begotten son, that whoever believes in Him will not perish but have everlasting life."

In Christ, the mystery of God's plan of redemption was fully revealed: God has always loved His human creation, and He always had a plan for their redemption.

His plan was to give His Son as a substitutionary sacrifice so that all who believed on Him would become heirs and joint heirs with Christ. Paul wrote: "In Him also we have obtained an inheritance." We are included in the "all things," both on earth and in heaven, which will be gathered together as one in Christ forever and ever. Here Paul again uses the word predestined. In this case, he says those who first believed in Jesus Christ — and he includes himself among that number — were predestined to be the means by which praise is brought to the glory of God. Because of the glory brought to God through His work in the lives of the earlier believers and because of their witness, the Ephesians were also brought to faith in Christ and have, together with the early believers, received the inheritance guaranteed by the presence of the Holy Spirit in their hearts.

The mystery is revealed. God loves us. He has provided for our redemption in Christ, and all believers, regardless of racial or ethnic background, are predestined to share the inheritance with the Son forever.

In the Meantime

I grew up in the days when the radio was the primary in-home entertainment medium. I listened to a lot of shows about the old West, and one of my favorite transition lines was "Meanwhile, back at the ranch ..." After giving the Ephesians a look at the eternal future of all believers, Paul then turns their attention to the present: "Meantime, back here on earth." In other words, "What can we expect while we are waiting on the day we will all be gathered together in Christ before the throne of God in heaven?" To explain, Paul used the words "sealed" and "guarantee."

Sealed

Sealed is a significant word. To be sealed carried the connotation of being hidden. A letter or other document was sealed to keep the things written inside secret and protected from those who would destroy or alter the contents. Psalm 91:1-2 carries this same sense. "He who dwells in the secret place of the Most High shall abide under the shadow of the Almighty. I will say of the LORD, 'He is my refuge and my fortress; My God, in Him will I trust.'" This theme of being "safely hidden" is carried forward in verses 9 and 10. "Because you have made the LORD, who is my refuge, even the Most High your dwelling place, no evil shall befall you, nor shall any plague come near your dwelling."

To be sealed could also be a sign of ownership. In the days of the Roman Empire, a seal might take the form of a tattoo or a brand. In the Jewish culture, one who chose to become a voluntary permanent bondservant would have his ear pierced with an awl. This piercing was probably to allow for the insertion of an earring as a sign of his status.

The term "sealed" also might refer to "posted property." A landowner may post his property with "No Trespassing" signs to keep hunters or vagrants from coming onto his land. If someone were caught on posted property, he could be fined or even sent to jail. If the property wasn't posted, hunters and others could feel free to enter the property to pursue their own purposes.

We are God's posted property, and Satan has no right to trespass on God's property. He has no right to take anything from us because we are under God's seal. While "No Trespassing" signs can be ignored, God's seal is an impenetrable barrier unless we, by disobedience to God, open the door and give Satan access.

Sealing also has to do with authentication and verification of authority. A document may carry a seal to verify its authenticity. The seal is a guarantee that the contents actually reflect the will of the writer and that it indeed came from the source claimed.

The seal represents power to act on the behalf of and according to the will of another. We have been given such authority to act on behalf of and according to the will of another. We are sealed by the Holy Spirit, and the Spirit's seal enables us to act on behalf of our Lord and guarantees the results of our actions.

For example, Jesus said, "In My name they will cast out demons; they will speak with new tongues; they will take up serpents and if they drink any deadly thing it will by no means harm them" (Mark 16:17, 18).

In the same vein, Jesus said in Acts 1:8, "You shall receive power [authority, authentication, be sealed] after the Holy Spirit has come upon you and you will be witnesses unto me ..."

Guarantee

The Holy Spirit, Who is our refuge and hiding place and our sign of ownership, is also our guarantee of the fulfillment of every promise of God in Jesus Christ.

This "guarantee" is what we would call a binder, a down payment or earnest money. When all parties have agreed to a transaction, the buyer will give the seller a small payment which represents and is a guarantee of the full payment to come. The earnest money binds both parties to what they have agreed upon. Neither can cancel the transaction without the consent of the other. This "guarantee" can also be viewed as a pledge that can be redeemed or as a ticket which assures admittance to a performance.

The Holy Spirit is our "down payment." He is our guarantee of eternal life in Christ with God. He is given to every believer as absolute assurance that everything God has promised to us in Christ will certainly come to fulfillment. Our complete inheritance includes:

1. Justification (counted as sinless)
2. Freedom from condemnation (no guilt)
3. Freedom from the power of sin and death (life free from the dominion of sin)
4. Sanctification (completely dedicated to God's holy purposes)
5. Righteousness (clothed in the righteousness of Christ)
6. Eternal life (in the presence of God forever)

7. Created anew (born again from above, given a new nature)
8. Perfect union with Christ
9. Perfect union with other believers
10. Eternal glory

God, by the gift of the Holy Spirit, has bound Himself and will not back out of the deal He has made with us in Christ. We are His, and He has committed Himself to making us heirs with His Son to all He has and is. Jesus spoke of this guarantee in John 10:29-30: "My sheep hear My voice and I know them, and they follow Me. And I will give them eternal life and they shall never perish, neither shall anyone snatch them out of My hand. My Father who has given them to Me is greater than all. No one is able to snatch them out of My hand. I and My Father are one."

The human factor is the only variable in this equation. The only condition to this security of the believer, the only way this guarantee can be voided, is for the believer to deliberately choose to live his life in continual disobedience to the voice of his Lord. Jesus knows His sheep, and He makes sure His voice reaches them, but following His voice seems to be a choice we must continue to make. John confirmed this truth when he wrote, "He that keeps his commandments dwells in him" (John 3:24). "Whoever continues to sin and does not abide in the doctrine of Christ does not know God" (2 John 1:9).

The "mystery" is revealed. In Christ, Jewish and Gentile believers alike are inheritors of all the riches of

CHAPTER 4

God. We are sealed by the Holy Spirit, and He is the down payment on the riches of our inheritance. His presence in us is the guarantee of delivery of the fullness of God to everyone who believes on Jesus Christ, the perfect sacrifice for our sins.

Chapter 5
A Prayer for the Church

Ephesians 1:15-19a:

Wherefore I also, after I heard of your faith in the Lord Jesus, and love unto all the saints, [16]Cease not to give thanks for you, making mention of you in my prayers; [17]That the God of our Lord Jesus Christ, the Father of glory, may give unto you the spirit of wisdom and revelation in the knowledge of him: [18]The eyes of your understanding being enlightened; that ye may know what is the hope of his calling, and what the riches of the glory of his inheritance in the saints, [19]And what is the exceeding greatness of his power to usward who believe (KJV).

Throughout the writings of Paul, we frequently find he includes spontaneous prayers and recitations of prayers he has prayed before on behalf of those to whom he is writing.

Paul's writings also contain a number of doxologies. A doxology is an effusive outpouring of praise to God. While it may not be part of a formal definition, the doxologies written by Paul seem to be spontaneous rather than well thought out. They just seem to erupt out of him because he is suddenly overwhelmed by his understanding of God and His purposes. It is as if in the course of explaining

CHAPTER 5

some spiritual truth, a fresh insight into the love and grace of God produces these short bursts of extravagant praise.

In the verses above, we find first a prayer, then a doxology. Something in Paul's prayer for the Ephesians apparently triggered this outburst of praise. As we look at the content of that prayer, we will begin to see what Paul saw and come to a new understanding of the awesomeness of God.

An Offering of Thanksgiving

Paul begins this prayer for the Ephesian church with thanksgiving, for their faith was well-known. Their love for one another was great, indicating that they understood that love of God was inseparably tied to love of the brethren. We should understand that there is no implied criticism of the Ephesians in Paul's prayer for them. Often when we pray we have in mind a deficiency or an inadequacy that needs to be corrected. In Paul's prayer for the Ephesians, we get the sense that while he recognized that they are already blessed, he prayed that they will receive even more blessing.

A Prayer for Understanding

After a brief statement of thanksgiving, Paul continued by praying that God would give them the "spirit of wisdom and revelation in the knowledge of Him (Jesus)." This "knowledge of Him" refers to all the things he has just recited as being the benefit of the Ephesian believer's position in Christ. His prayer is that they will come into a full understanding of what they have already received in Him.

In Him, they have redemption and forgiveness of sin.

In Him, the mystery of the will of God has been made known.

In Him, all things will be gathered together.

In Him, they have obtained an eternal inheritance.

In Him, they are sealed with the Holy Spirit of promise.

All these things Paul freely acknowledges that the Ephesians have received through faith in Jesus Christ. Paul does not imply that the Ephesians have a deficit in any of these things. Neither is his prayer that they will receive more of these things, for in Christ these things are already complete. His prayer was that they would come to understand — have full comprehension of — the extent of their privileges and position in Christ. He prayed that a spirit of wisdom would be theirs to bring the fullness of this knowledge. He prayed for a spirit of revelation and that the eyes of their heart would be enlightened. He prayed that their knowledge and understanding would be increased in three specific areas:

1. The hope of their calling;
2. The riches of His inheritance in the saints; and
3. The exceeding greatness of God's power at work for the benefit of those who believe.

Chapter 5

<u>The Hope of His Calling</u>

In Romans 8:30, we find that those whom God has called, He also justified, and those He justified, He also glorified. The hope of the Christian is the certainty of a radically altered future.

The "Great Hope" of the church is the bodily resurrection which precedes our entry into eternal life in the presence of God. This hope is centered in the fact that Christ Himself is resurrected. Because Christ was raised from the dead, we have the guarantee that all who believe in Him and follow Him faithfully will also be raised from the dead. We will not be raised up in the same condition as before, but in new and perfect bodies, not subject to death, disease or destruction. Not only will our resurrection bodies be perfect, but so will our soul and spirit. We will be raised up not only in the same manner as Christ, but we will also share in His perfection. "We will be like Him, because we will see Him as He is."

Our hope extends even beyond these marvelous conditions. We are destined to spend our never-ending, ever-perfect existence in the eternal presence of God, where there is fullness of joy. This is the unalterable destiny and certain hope of all who believe and walk as disciples of Christ.

<u>The Riches of His Inheritance</u>

The next section in this prayer, at first glance, may seem to refer to our inheritance as saints, the inheritance which was just described under the heading of our hope.

However, this statement actually refers to God's inheritance which is identified as being "in the saints." "The saints" refers to the church and every member of the body of Christ. According to this passage, the inheritance of God is the church.

This statement points to a truth that is frequently overlooked. God's greatest glory is yet to come. God's greatest work is yet to be accomplished. God's greatest work, the accomplishment that will bring Him the greatest honor and glory, is not the creation of the universe or even man himself. God's greatest work and the thing that will be held in the greatest awe throughout all eternity will be the redemption of mankind.

Peter wrote that even the angels don't really understand God's redemptive plan. The same theme crops up in the Book of Revelation where we see the saints singing the song of the redeemed from which the angels are excluded. We are God's inheritance. God's redemption of mankind, motivated by His incomprehensible love for us, will be the theme of our praise and worship throughout all eternity. The sense of awe that we and the angels will share over His redeeming grace will never diminish.

All this emphasizes how precious each believer is in the eyes of God. We are His inheritance. We were redeemed for His glory. His eternal glory is enhanced by our salvation. God is committed to us and to our redemption. He has called us. As Jesus said, "You have not chosen Me, I have chosen you." He has justified us and declared us not guilty of sin. He has made us righteous and acceptable to Himself by His only begotten Son, and He has committed Himself to our sanctification, which will be to His glory forever.

The Greatness of His Power

The third element of the understanding for which Paul prays is that the Ephesians would know "what was the exceeding greatness of His power toward those who believe."

The Bible teaches us that although we have been justified through Christ's sacrifice, and we will be glorified to the eternal glory of the Father, there is still that period between justification and glorification of sanctification, or the process by which the image of Christ is developed in and displayed by the believer. Sanctification is the natural outgrowth of justification and is necessary for our ultimate glorification.

This is what Paul wants the Ephesians to understand, the absolutely incredible power of God that is at work in every believer to preserve, protect and perfect. God is committed to our sanctification because He loves us and because we are His inheritance. In Ephesians 2:6-7, Paul states that God has "… raised us up together in the heavenly places in Christ Jesus, that in the ages to come we might show the exceeding riches of His grace in His kindness toward us."

God's power is at work to preserve us. The Scriptures are full of references to God's preserving power. Proverbs

2:8 reads, "He keeps the paths of judgment and preserves the way of the saints." Isaiah reminds us that "no weapon fashioned against you shall be successful." Paul consistently affirms this truth, "If God be for us, who can be against us?" "With every temptation He has made a way of escape that you may be able to bear it." Paul assured Timothy of God's protecting power when he wrote, "And the Lord shall deliver you from every evil work and will preserve you unto His heavenly kingdom." This is an excellent example of the grace of God, which can be defined as "God at work on our behalf, all the time."

God's power is at work to protect us. There is only a shade of difference between God's protection and His preservation. John reminds us of Jesus' personal commitment to our protection. "These things I have spoken to you that you might have peace: in the world you will have tribulation but be of good cheer, I have overcome the world" (John 16:33). Paul referred to this protection later in this letter when he wrote, "Finally, my brethren, be strong in the Lord and in the power of His might. Put on the whole armor of God that you may be able to stand against the wiles of the devil." God is committed to protecting us.

God's power is at work to perfect us. Again, the Scriptures are replete with God's promises to perfect us. Philippians 1:6 reads, "For He is at work in you both to will and to do of His good pleasure." God gives us both the desire and the ability to live in a way that pleases and

Chapter 5

brings glory to Him and His Son. Paul wants the Ephesians to be ever conscious of God's power at work in them to develop Christ's image in them, because He has predestined them to be conformed to the image of His Son. He expands on this theme in a later part of this letter. "Christ also loved the church [and each individual member of it] and gave Himself for her that He might sanctify her and cleanse her by the washing of water by the word, that He might present her to Himself; nor having spot or wrinkle or any such thing, but that she should be holy and without blemish" (Ephesians 5:25b-27).

The real problem is not inadequate provision for the Christian life, but an inadequate grasp of the extent of the provision God has already made.

CHAPTER 6
GOD'S POWER
DEMONSTRATED IN CHRIST

Ephesians 1:19b-23:

... according to the working of his mighty power, [20]Which he wrought in Christ, when he raised him from the dead, and set him at his own right hand in the heavenly places, [21]Far above all principality, and power, and might, and dominion, and every name that is named, not only in this world, but also in that which is to come: [22]And hath put all things under his feet, and gave him to be the head over all things to the church, [23]Which is his body, the fulness of him that filleth all in all (KJV).

Paul continued his prayer by asking that the Ephesians would receive a revelation of what God's power had already wrought in Christ. It is as if Paul was thinking, "If they can understand what God has already done through Christ, then perhaps that will enable them to come into an understanding of what God yet desires to do in them."

He, first of all, refers to the greatest demonstration of God's power since the creation of the universe, the resurrection of Jesus from the dead. The significance of the resurrection as a witness to the power of God cannot be overstated. Although there are many examples of people being raised from the dead in both the Old and

Chapter 6

New Testaments, the resurrection of Jesus was a totally unprecedented occurrence. Everyone who had been raised from the dead before the resurrection of Jesus had eventually died again. The body in which they were raised was the same body in which they had died. Life had returned to the body, but it was the same kind of body, subject to the same forces of disease and death which had caused its death in the first place. With Jesus, it was entirely different.

Jesus was resurrected to a whole new form of life. In appearance, He was the same as before. Even the scars of His crucifixion were still evident in His hands, feet and side. He still ate and drank. He still walked and talked.

But yet, He was different. His body was no longer subject to injury, disease or death. His new body had abilities Jesus had never demonstrated before. He could apparently transport Himself instantly from one location to another, appearing and disappearing at will. Jesus could also freely move from earth to heaven and back and continued to do so until He ascended visibly and for the last time into heaven. There God seated Him at His right hand.

In this position, Jesus assumed obvious superiority over every other power in the universe, both in the present and for all time to come.

Some Jews believed that angels controlled the destiny of humanity, so it was important for the Ephesians to understand that Jesus is superior to all creation, including all angelic and demonic beings. Jesus, being the uncreated

One, equal to and eternally co-existent with the Father, has lordship over all. It is He alone who has authority in the life of a Christian.

John 5:27 tells us Jesus has been given "authority to execute judgment." God sent Jesus to earth to be our Savior, but having accomplished the work of salvation, He is now placed in the position of Judge of all, and for all mankind, His judgment will be based on how each individual responded to His sacrifice.

Paul also makes reference to the name which God gave Jesus, "a name above every name." In Jewish culture, a person's name had great significance. Their name was representative of their personhood. Their name represented all they were and all they had done. At times a name was prophetic of what a child would become. Perhaps the name God gave Jesus, as He assumed His position at God's right hand, is the name we read about in Revelation 19:6: "And He has on His robe and on His thigh a name written: 'KING OF KINGS AND LORD OF LORDS.'"

As he continued to emphasize Jesus' authority, Paul used yet another metaphor. "He (the Father) has put everything under His feet, and gave Him to be head over all things to the church." This creates an interesting picture. Everything in all creation is placed under the feet of Jesus, but the church is in a special position, not under His feet, but under His head. The inference certainly can be taken that in Christ, we, too, have authority over all the forces of the enemy. God is able to do His work in us

CHAPTER 6

through His Son, and no other power has the authority to interfere with the accomplishment of God's purposes in us.

Paul's motive for the recitation of all the things that God has accomplished in Christ is to have the Ephesians come to fully understand that God has already begun and desires to complete like things in them.

Christ is raised from the dead, and all who believe on Him already have eternal life, even though they still face physical death. The impermanence of physical death of the body is the "Great Hope" of the church. Romans 8:6 declares, "If we be dead with Christ; we believe that we shall also live with Him." Paul also wrote to the Thessalonian church that "the dead in Christ shall rise first." Both passages bring assurance that physical death is not permanent, but just as Jesus rose from the dead to a new form of life in a physical body, so shall everyone who believes on Him.

The Ephesians were also made to understand that just as Jesus has been given a place of authority at the right hand of God, the church also will rule and reign with Christ, and God has raised us up together and made us to sit in a heavenly place in Christ Jesus. Although we are still, at this point, in the physical realm and bound to this earth, in the spiritual realm, we are already enjoying exaltation in Christ.

Chapter 7
Raised Up By Jesus

Ephesians 2:1-9:

And you hath he quickened, who were dead in trespasses and sins; [2]Wherein in time past ye walked according to the course of this world, according to the prince of the power of the air, the spirit that now worketh in the children of disobedience: [3]Among whom also we all had our conversation in times past in the lusts of our flesh, fulfilling the desires of the flesh and of the mind; and were by nature the children of wrath, even as others. [4]But God, who is rich in mercy, for his great love wherewith he loved us, [5]Even when we were dead in sins, hath quickened us together with Christ, (by grace ye are saved;) [6]And hath raised us up together, and made us sit together in heavenly places in Christ Jesus: [7]That in the ages to come he might shew the exceeding riches of his grace in his kindness toward us through Christ Jesus. [8]For by grace are ye saved through faith; and that not of yourselves: it is the gift of God: [9]Not of works, lest any man should boast (KJV).

A few years ago there was a song that referred to the fact that God has raised us up in Christ to be more than we could ever be on our own. Paul wrote that "If we die with Him, we will also be raised up to new life in Him." We can experience being raised up with Christ in a number of ways. This passage reveals three of them: raised from sin, raised to righteousness and raised to good works.

Raised From Sin

First and foremost, we have been raised from the death imposed by our sin. "And you He made alive who were dead in trespasses and sin."

While we say we believe that every human being is born spiritually dead, what we seem to actually practice is that every human being is born with a nature that will inevitably produce sinful behavior. Therefore, we can say that babies are born in a state of innocence, and should they die in infancy, they will return to their heavenly Father.

However, every child is born with a sin nature that will inevitably produce disobedience to God, not eventually, but at the first possible opportunity. Consequently, when Paul writes to the Romans that "All have sinned and come short of the glory of God" (Romans 3:23), we can affirm our belief in the truth of that statement. The only possible exception is a person who, even as an adult, is so mentally challenged they are not able to conceptualize right and wrong.

It is by the grace of God made available to us through the death of our Savior that we who have believed on Jesus have passed from death unto life.

It is imperative that we understand the larger connotation of the words "believe" and "grace."

To believe, as it applies to salvation through Jesus Christ, means so much more than agreeing that a certain set of facts is true.

To believe in someone means to become a disciple of the one in whom you believe. To be a disciple means that you devote yourself to the lifestyle and philosophy of the one in whom you believe. In ancient Greek culture, philosophers such as Plato and Socrates gathered disciples about them, and what distinguished their disciples was the fact that they lived their lives in accordance with the philosophy of their teacher. The same must be true of disciples of Christ.

By faith in Christ's sacrifice, we who were spiritually dead — separated from God in this life and in the life to come — have become reconciled unto God. Just as Jesus is forever in the presence of His Father, we who are in Christ are also forever guaranteed a place in the presence of God. In Christ, we are with the Father and will always be with Him, so for the believer, the specter of spiritual death no longer exists.

Even physical death is only a rite of passage because "to be absent from the body is to be present with the Lord." When Jesus returns, those who have died in faith and have subsequently been living in the presence of God will come out of the grave and be caught up together with all the saints to inhabit heaven forever in their resurrected bodies.

From the moment we believed in Jesus, we were given new life in the here and now. It is not something for which we must wait. The expression of this new life will change, but all believers are in possession of this gift.

Raised to Righteousness

Resurrection from the death of sin and the gift of eternal life has been granted to us by God because we believed in His Son's sacrifice. At the same time, we are given the righteousness of Christ. The righteousness of Christ is an unearned, undeserved gift.

There is a saying, "You are not a sinner because you sin; you sin because you are a sinner." It's the same as saying, "A dog acts like a dog, because it is a dog." A sinner acts like a sinner, because he is a sinner. When we are saved, justified, given the righteousness of Christ, we become new creatures in Christ. We have been given righteous status before God, and we are given a new nature which will enable us to live our lives in a new way. We are enabled to be producers of righteousness rather than producers of sinfulness.

Before we were saved, we might be able to do good things, but we were not able to be righteous because being righteous requires faith. Even after we are saved, we still have no capability to produce righteousness, because all our righteousness will forever be in Christ, not in our works. Good works never produce righteousness, but a consistent outflow of good works can come from one who has been granted the righteousness of Christ.

Not only have believers been granted a position of righteousness before God, we have also been given the

Spirit of Christ, the Holy Spirit, by which we can begin to consistently display the fruit of the Spirit: love, joy, peace, longsuffering, kindness, goodness, faithfulness, gentleness and self-control (Galatians 5:22 NKJV).

We are pleasing to God because of the righteousness of Christ that we have been given. While as a sinner one can do good works, these good works can never please God. All that ever pleases God is action in obedience to the Spirit of God.

Raised to Good Works

We are raised from sin to righteousness, and as a result of Christ's righteousness, we are raised to good works. God has a lifetime plan of good works laid out for every believer. The accomplishment of this plan depends on the believer's obedience.

Obedience to God obviously will involve the avoidance of sin, but Christian obedience involves more than keeping the Ten Commandments and the other corollary commandments which the Bible contains. While there are many biblical "Thou shalt nots" and "Thou shalts" which apply equally to all believers, God has a specific plan of action for each believer which has nothing to do with what we think of as "sinning" or "not sinning." This God-ordained program of good works involves things that God will call each one specifically and individually to do.

For example, while "Thou shalt not steal" is a general command and applies to everyone, "I want you to teach the junior boy's Sunday school class" is a command to the individual alone. To obey this specific command is to do a "good work"; to disobey is a sin for the one who receives the call. In like manner, "Go into all the world and preach the gospel" is a general command to every believer, whereas "Go witness to John next door" is a specific call which no one else may receive.

Few people feel adequate to accomplish the specifics of God's plan for their lives. They doubt their ability to do these "good works." However, as the old saying goes, "God does not call the equipped, He equips the called."

For example, Moses certainly had his weak points. He was a murderer, and he had a speech impediment, yet God raised him up to do mighty works.

Peter certainly would not seem qualified for the great role he was to play in the growth of the church. He was a braggart, impetuous and denied Christ three times. Yet he, too, God raised up to do great good works.

Paul was a persecutor of the church, killing Christians and putting them in prison. Although he was apparently highly educated, he was not an eloquent speaker, and there are hints in the Scripture that he may have been considerably less than handsome, perhaps afflicted with a physical deformity and weak eyes. But God raised him up to good works, and we are even now, about 2,000 years later, studying one of the works to which God raised him up.

CHAPTER 8
GOD'S POETIC MASTERPIECE

Ephesians 2:10:
For we are his workmanship, created in Christ Jesus unto good works, which God hath before ordained that we should walk in them (KJV).

In verse 10, the word "workmanship" appears. This word, which is a translation of the Greek word "poiema," carries the meaning of something created or crafted by a highly skilled artisan. It is the word from which the English words "poem" and "poetry" are derived. Therefore, it would seem appropriate to think of God's workmanship as being His poem or His poetic masterpiece.

Many people are able to produce a bit of doggerel, but it takes a true master to create a poem that is not only enjoyed by the poet's contemporaries, but by generations to come. Poetry is in fact a form of verbal art. Shakespeare, Robert and Elizabeth Browning, Walt Whitman and Henry Wadsworth Longfellow are examples of verbal artists whose works survived and bring blessings long after their deaths.

The church is God's workmanship; the church is God's poetic masterpiece, and each individual member of the body of Christ is intended to be a poem within a poem. Therefore, everyone can say that we each are God's workmanship, His design, His artistic product. He has brought order, rhythm and beauty into our lives, and His creativity displayed in us brings honor and glory to Him in the world.

Without Form and Void

Our lives before we were converted were in chaos, like words jumbled on a page. Before Christ came in, there was little order and less beauty. It was as if the poem of our life had been cut apart, word by word, jumbled together and then cast at random on the page. The pieces were all there, the words were present, but without the Master's workmanship to bring them into order, rhythm and rhyme, their beauty would never be realized.

The Bible calls this chaotic condition spiritual death. Spiritually, our lives were without form and void of meaning. The course of this spiritually dead world is set by the prince of the powers of the air, who is the enemy of our souls. Those who follow the course set by the devil are the sons of disobedience. This is another way of defining the condition of spiritual deadness into which we were all born.

Spiritual death means we have followed Satan in his rebellion against God and that we live our lives the way we want, rather than the way God desires. By following his lead, you get to pursue your own goals without regard for God and His purposes. Satan's big lie is that God is really unfair, and He wants to keep the really good things from you. Satan would have us believe that only by following our own way can we have the best that life has to offer.

Paul clearly states that we have all been in this state. We were all "children of disobedience among whom also we conducted ourselves in the lusts of the flesh, fulfilling the desires of the flesh and of the mind, and were by nature children of wrath" (Ephesians 2:2-3).

Spiritual death has as its major symptom the going of one's own way and fulfilling the desires of one's own flesh and mind without regard for the will of God.

Conformed to His Image

The workmanship that God creates is intended for "good works, which God has prepared beforehand that we should walk in them."

One might reasonably conclude that the meaning of this phrase is that God has laid out a course for each believer. Along this course there are a series of opportunities to do things that will contribute to the growth of the kingdom of God. Along this course we may choose to be obedient and do the good work or be disobedient and fail to take advantage of the opportunity. Reward and approval would follow the obedience, and disapproval and chastisement might very well follow the disobedience.

While there is no doubt of the validity of this interpretation, there is another way to look at this passage. Perhaps it means that for everyone God has made alive in Christ, He has laid out for Himself a series of "good works" that He is going to accomplish in that life. He knows what each believer's potential is, and He is committed to using the raw material placed in His hands to create a masterpiece that will reflect His glory and grace.

Some of His good work will bring us into conformity with the image of His Son. As He brings us into conformity to the likeness of Christ, we then become conduits through which He can show His glory and grace to others. As He shapes us into the image of Christ, He uses us to make His love known to the world around us.

This process occurs in the individual believer, as well as in the corporate body of the church. The shaping of the church into the bride of Christ, "without spot or wrinkle or any such thing," is not in any way a human accomplishment, but totally the work of God. Jesus sent His disciples into the world to preach the gospel, but He reserved the task of building His church to Himself. We are His workmanship, whether we look at His followers as individuals or as a corporate body.

God wants to make something beautiful of our lives for the purpose of bringing honor and glory to Himself. We are the medium in which He has chosen to accomplish His most honored work. As the sculptor works in stone, the painter works with canvas and paint or a poet works with words, God works in the medium of human hearts.

Of all the artistic media in the universe, human flesh is the only one which can resist the will of the artist.

However, despite their occasional resistance, all true believers are predestined to be conformed to the image of Christ.

CHAPTER 9
THE GENTILES CHANGED POSITION

Part 1: Remember From Where You Came

Ephesians 2:11-12:

Wherefore remember, that ye being in time past Gentiles in the flesh, who are called Uncircumcision by that which is called the Circumcision in the flesh made by hands; [12] That at that time ye were without Christ, being aliens from the commonwealth of Israel, and strangers from the covenants of promise, having no hope, and without God in the world: (KJV).

At this point in his letter, Paul began his discussion of the unity of all believers, Gentile and Jew, and their shared position in Christ. The first part of his discussion is directed to the Gentile believers. Later in the letter, he will direct his remarks to the Jewish believers. In this first part, Paul calls upon the Gentiles to: Remember from where you came, realize what Christ has done and rejoice in your present position.

Without Hope and Without God

Paul began Chapter 2 by saying, "And you He made alive, who were dead in trespasses and sins." The Ephesian church consisted of both Jews and Gentiles, and Paul initially directed his message to the church as a whole, reminding them of who they are in Christ and what He has done and is doing in them. At this point, beginning in verse 11, Paul seems to be addressing the two groups separately in order to emphasize that Christ's work was essentially the same in both the Jew and the Gentile.

As he reminds the Gentile Ephesians where they had come from, he does so from a Jewish perspective, because although the Jews did not always live in accordance with the covenant God had made with them, they were people of the covenant, something the Gentiles could never had said.

The Jews, who called themselves "The Circumcision," referred to the Gentiles as "the uncircumcised." This was a term of derision, alienation and contempt. The circumcision of all Jewish males was the sign of the covenant God had made with the children of Israel.

The Gentiles were aliens (strangers, foreigners) from the nation of Israel and had none of the blessings of God or of citizenship in national Israel. They were alienated from Israel and their God by their idolatry. They had no part in the Abrahamic covenant. They had no part in national or spiritual Israel. They were afar off; they were separated from Israel and her God.

The Gentiles had no equivalent understanding of the promise of redemption that was implicit in the covenant God made with Abraham, and having no "promise," they had no hope. They had no promise of pardon for their sin,

CHAPTER 9

nor the hope of resurrection. They had many "gods," but no knowledge of the true God and His Son. The Gentiles were lost. However, even though they had no awareness of it, God had always planned to have them share in all the promises and blessings of Israel through Jesus Christ Who had been revealed to them.

Part 2: Realize What Christ Has Done

Ephesians 2:13-18:

But now in Christ Jesus ye who sometimes were far off are made nigh by the blood of Christ. [14]For he is our peace, who hath made both one, and hath broken down the middle wall of partition between us; [15]Having abolished in his flesh the enmity, even the law of commandments contained in ordinances; for to make in himself of twain one new man, so making peace; [16]And that he might reconcile both unto God in one body by the cross, having slain the enmity thereby: [17]And came and preached peace to you which were afar off, and to them that were nigh. [18]For through him we both have access by one Spirit unto the Father (KJV).

Brought Near by the Blood of Jesus

The Jews considered themselves to be "near" to God, and all others were considered to be "afar off." Jews understood themselves to be God's special people by virtue of the special covenant He had made with the patriarchs. Everyone else was outside any covenant

67

relationship with God and was without hope in the world. The actual truth was that at the time Christ came, the Jews were about as far away from God as were the Gentiles in terms of true worship and understanding, but now both Jew and Gentile, by the blood of Jesus, were reconciled unto God by faith.

All Are One in Christ

Paul emphasized the oneness of all people in the body of Christ when he said that Christ is our peace. He is our peace because He has torn down all the barriers to full fellowship with Himself and all other people. He also speaks of Christ having torn down the "dividing wall of hostility" between the Jews and the Gentiles. This refers to the wall in the Temple Court which separated the Court of the Gentiles and the Court of Israel. This barrier kept Gentile worshippers of Yahweh separated from the Jewish worshippers and kept them at a distance from the holy precincts of the Temple.

All of this is symbolic of the fact that Christ had come to save all people as they believed on Him, Jew and Gentile alike. Now, in Christ, Jew and Gentile together are His body and one in Him. This is the "mystery" now being revealed. Christ had brought peace between the Christian of Jewish descent and the Christian of Gentile ancestry, and Paul is endeavoring to make them see that they are no longer Jews or Gentiles, but "new creations" in Christ. Since Christ had completed the work of salvation, in God's eyes, the world consisted of believers and non-believers and, in the church, brothers and sisters in Christ. In the church, there is no more male and female, slave or free, Jew or Gentile, but all are equal before God as members of the body of Christ.

This unity is possible because Christ has in His flesh abolished the Law, which was the reason for the enmity between the Jew and the Gentile. The Law was completely fulfilled by Christ; therefore, all who believe on Jesus and walk in the Spirit are also seen by God to have fulfilled the Law.

When we speak of the Law in this context, it must be understood that it is only the ceremonial parts of the Mosaic Law that is in view. In the Bible, we have revealed essentially two different types of God's law. First, we see the laws that were prophetic depictions of the work Jesus would do by His life ministry, death and resurrection. For instance, the laws that related to the different kinds of animal sacrifices would be considered ceremonial. These are null and void for the Christian because Jesus fulfilled all those requirements by His death.

Then, second, we have to take into account the moral laws of God. These are the behavioral mandates that reflect the nature and character of God. These laws, which are to regulate our behavior toward other people and God Himself, are not ceremonial but moral and were not nullified by the work of Christ. These laws are still in effect and apply to Christian and non-Christian alike.

Not only did God abolish the enmity between Jew and Gentile, He, according to Colossians 1:20, abolished the enmity that had existed between God and man. Enmity is the feeling enemies have toward each other: separation, hatred and discord. In Christ, peace was now established between God and all who would believe on Jesus. In Christ, all separation, hatred and discord are removed between God and man.

Jesus came and preached to the Jew, those who were near, and to the Gentiles, those who were afar off, and reconciled them both to God through His sacrifice on the cross. Through the Holy Spirit, Whom Jesus sent to be our Comforter, both Jew and Gentile have access to the Father.

Part 3: Rejoice in Your Present Position

Ephesians 2:19-22:

Now therefore ye are no more strangers and foreigners, but fellow citizens with the saints, and of the household of God; [20] And are built upon the foundation of the apostles and prophets, Jesus Christ himself being the chief corner stone; [21] In whom all the building fitly framed together groweth unto an holy temple in the Lord: [22] In whom ye also are builded together for an habitation of God through the Spirit (KJV).

Paul explained the Gentile's new position in Christ, which they shared with the Jews, using three different metaphors. In the first, he compares their position to a change in citizenship. In the second, he likens them to a family, and in the third, he compares them to a building.

CHAPTER 9

Gentiles had no rights as citizens in Israel. As heathens, or "strangers," they were not granted the right to own property in Israel, nor were they allowed to enter the social or religious life of nation, except on a very limited basis. They could become "sojourners," those who worshipped the God of Israel, but they were not circumcised, and they were still excluded from true fellowship with the Jews. However, in Christ, they have equal citizenship rights with the Jews in the kingdom of God.

Next Paul uses the metaphor of the family. The Jews considered themselves alone to be the household of God, or members of the family of God, but now, in Christ, the Gentiles have also been included. The privilege of being of the "household of faith" has been made available to all mankind.

Last, Paul likens the unified body of Christ to a building. The body of Christ is like a building constructed of individual stones with Jesus being the Chief Cornerstone. The cornerstone was essential to the construction of a stone building. The cornerstone had to be perfect in dimension and alignment. Every other stone in the structure was subsequently aligned with the cornerstone. As Christian believers, we are to be in alignment with Jesus Who is our foundation. It is He who sets the standard to which our lives must measure up.

Peter also uses the metaphor of the church as a building of stones and Jesus as the Cornerstone. "Coming to Him as to a living stone, rejected indeed by men, but chosen by God and precious, ⁵you also, as living stones, are being built up a spiritual house, a holy priesthood, to offer up spiritual sacrifices acceptable to God through Jesus Christ. ⁶Therefore it is also contained in the Scripture, 'Behold, I lay in Zion a chief cornerstone, elect, precious, and he who believes on Him will by no means be put to shame'" (1Peter 2:4-6).

The Temple of God is no longer the stone structure that occupied the central place in the city of Jerusalem. The temple of God is now the church, made up of all believers in Jesus Christ, without regard for their racial or cultural background. It is in the church that the Holy Spirit dwells.

When the dwelling place of the Holy Spirit is mentioned, we must be careful to understand whether it is the individual indwelling or the corporate indwelling that is meant. We tend to assume that the individual is always in view, however, the corporate dwelling, which is the body of Christ, can also be in view. When Paul talked about abstaining from sin, he said, "Don't you know that your body is the temple of the Holy Spirit?" The individual is clearly in mind, however, when Jesus said, "Where two or three are gathered together in My name, I will be in the midst of them," He referred to a different dimension of His presence, which would be manifested only when the body of Christ is assembled.

The church is not merely a group of independent individuals in whom the Spirit dwells. The Spirit transcends the confines of the individual bodies and indwells and ties together members of the local assembly and the entire corporate body of believers worldwide.

Therefore, division in the body of Christ is not acceptable to God and cannot be rationalized on any basis. In Christ, God has brought all believers together into one. Any attempt to divide the body of Christ into sects or classes is a clear violation of the work of Christ and the will of God.

CHAPTER 10
PAUL CALLS FOR JEWS TO ACCEPT THE GENTILES

Ephesians 3:1-13:

For this cause I Paul, the prisoner of Jesus Christ for you Gentiles, [2] If ye have heard of the dispensation of the grace of God which is given me to youward, [3] How that by revelation he made known unto me the mystery; (as I wrote afore in few words, [4] Whereby, when ye read, ye may understand my knowledge in the mystery of Christ) [5] Which in other ages was not made known unto the sons of men, as it is now revealed unto his holy apostles and prophets by the Spirit; [6] That the Gentiles should be fellow heirs, and of the same body, and partakers of his promise in Christ by the gospel: [7] Whereof I was made a minister, according to the gift of the grace of God given unto me by the effectual working of his power. [8] Unto me, who am less than the least of all saints, is this grace given, that I should preach among the Gentiles the unsearchable riches of Christ; [9] And to make all men see what is the fellowship of the mystery, which from the beginning of the world hath been hid in God, who created all things by Jesus Christ: [10] To the intent that now unto the principalities and powers in heavenly places might be known by the church the manifold wisdom of God, [11] According to the eternal purpose which he purposed in Christ Jesus our Lord: [12] In whom we have boldness and access with confidence by the faith of him. [13] *Wherefore I desire that ye faint not at my tribulations for you, which is your glory (KJV).*

Paul's Administration of Grace

In this segment of his Letter to the Ephesians, Paul continues to discuss the "mystery of Christ." Building on the foundation he has already laid, he continues to build on the theme of the mystery of God's will, plan and purposes which had been previously hidden and which were now revealed through the person and ministry of Jesus Christ. At this point, Paul's discussion of the "mystery" seems to be directed more toward Jewish believers rather than the Gentiles.

Paul considered himself a prisoner, not of the Romans, but of the Lord Jesus Christ. In fact, he considered himself to have been Christ's slave ever since his Damascus Road experience. His primary calling was to be the apostle to the Gentiles. However, whenever he would go into a new city, he would almost always go to the Jews first and teach in the synagogue, until their rejection of the gospel left him no alternative but to establish a church among the Gentiles.

Paul was called to proclaim the "mystery of Christ," which he had received by special revelation from Christ, and in verse 6, we find a concise statement of that mystery which had been previously unknown (in a general sense), but was now made abundantly clear: "... that the Gentiles should be fellow heirs of the same body and partakers of

His (that is, God's) promises in Christ through the gospel."

The Jewish Perspective

There were several sects of Judaism at the time of Christ and following. The most prominent were the Pharisees and the Sadducees. The Sadducees were a liberal group, which did not believe in angels, spirits or resurrection from the dead. The Pharisees believed in all these things, and early Christianity adopted, to a large extent, the Pharisees' view of Old Testament theology.

Although the Jewish belief system was not completely homogeneous, for the most part, they believed that only they and those who became Jews by the provisions of the Law of Moses would escape eternal damnation. They uniformly believed themselves to have a unique and exclusive relationship with Yahweh. At the time of Christ, the Jews believed that paradise was reserved for the righteous Jews, and all others, including non-observant Jews and Gentiles, would be consigned without hope to the fiery pit whose flames were never extinguished. This belief system carried over into the early church, which was almost entirely composed of Jewish believers. One of the earliest and most consistent battles that raged in the early church was with the "Judaizers," who insisted that in order to become a Christian, one must first become an observant Jew.

Although the Jews had missed it and it had become a "mystery" to them, the concept of God's salvation being extended to all the people of the earth was never completely hidden. In fact, God's initial call to Abraham included the promise, "And in you all the families of the earth shall be blessed" (Genesis 12:3).

Throughout the history of God's dealing with the Jews, God's intention to extend salvation to all the nations of the earth surfaces clearly from time to time. For instance, Isaiah wrote, "The people that walked in darkness have seen a great light" (Isaiah 9:2). This specifically refers to the Gentiles coming to know the Jewish Messiah as their Savior. He also wrote, "I will give you for a light to the Gentiles" (Isaiah 49:6). This is an allusion to the fact that God intended the Israelites to demonstrate His power and love to the world around them and be His witness to the nations. As a nation, the Jews never accomplished this to any great extent, but when Jesus came and His disciples went out to the whole world to preach the "Good News," the light of the gospel did go out from the Jews to the Gentiles.

Jesus confirmed that the Gentiles were to be included in the church when He told His disciples to "Go into all the world and preach the gospel to every creature." His kingdom, His church, would not consist of believing Jews only, but would consist of everyone, regardless of heritage, race or nationality, who would believe on His name and become His disciples. Thus, Jesus affirmed the universality of God's plan of salvation.

This "mystery," this hidden truth that the plan of God was to extend salvation to the Gentiles, was again brought to light when Peter was called to preach the gospel to the Gentiles at Cornelius' house. Peter, before this incident, had preached the gospel to the Jews only, but on this occasion was led by the Holy Spirit through a series of visions to go to the house of this Roman Centurion and preach the gospel to those assembled there. As Peter preached to them of Jesus, God confirmed His intention to include Jews and Gentiles in the church of Jesus Christ on an equal footing by pouring out the Holy Spirit upon the Gentiles in the same manner in which His Spirit had been poured out on the Jews on the Day of Pentecost.

Despite this clear evidence to the contrary, the Jews continued to promote the idea that Gentile believers were and always would be inferior to Jewish believers. Paul felt it was an integral part of his ministry to proclaim as an essential part of the gospel that "the Gentiles should be fellow heirs, of the same body, and partakers of the promise in Christ through the gospel."

The Unified Church Declares God's Glory

Paul felt compelled to bring the "Good News" to the Gentiles. This was why Paul was called and fitted to be a minister. This was the administration of grace given to Paul, and therefore, it had become his purpose to share with all men what had been revealed to him. He did not consider himself to be worthy of the revelation, but by grace he had been given the privilege of making God's eternal plan known to the Gentiles and thus include them in the church.

Chapter 10

In turn, the church would go on to display before all the evil principalities and powers His means of carrying the gospel to the entire world. The message of the gospel preached through the church would be the means by which evil would be defeated and God's kingdom established in the hearts of men. This was His eternal purpose which had now been accomplished through the work of Christ. Knowing this, even though his current circumstances are not good, Paul had boldness and confidence to continue to minister. Even though severely tried, Paul had not lost heart. Citing his confidence, Paul challenged the Ephesians to also not lose heart because his trials for them would ultimately result in heavenly rewards, which they would share with him.

CHAPTER 11
A PRAYER
FOR THE CHURCH

Ephesians 3:14-21:

For this cause I bow my knees unto the Father of our Lord Jesus Christ, [15] Of whom the whole family in heaven and earth is named, [16] That he would grant you, according to the riches of his glory, to be strengthened with might by his Spirit in the inner man; [17] That Christ may dwell in your hearts by faith; that ye, being rooted and grounded in love, [18] May be able to comprehend with all saints what is the breadth, and length, and depth, and height; [19] And to know the love of Christ, which passeth knowledge, that ye might be filled with all the fulness of God. [20] Now unto him that is able to do exceeding abundantly above all that we ask or think, according to the power that worketh in us, [21] Unto him be glory in the church by Christ Jesus throughout all ages, world without end. Amen (KJV).

Paul's Second Prayer

In the beginning of his letter, he prayed that they might gain knowledge of what God had done for them in Christ Jesus. This prayer focuses on their need for strength and power and consists of four separate elements, each of which is introduced by the word "that."

First, he prayed, "That He would grant you, according

CHAPTER 11

to the riches of His glory, to be strengthened with might through His Spirit in the inner man." Paul's concern is that they would recognize the awesome and unlimited power that God possesses and that He is able to exert on their behalf. God has given to every believer His Holy Spirit, and the Spirit lives in them to empower them for righteous living and Christian witness.

This passage anticipates the exposition on the "whole armor of God" in Chapter 6, which is a picture of the strength to resist the evil one which is available to all those who are in Christ. The believer is equipped for victory, but even the most powerful weapons available for any battle are ineffective if there is no awareness of the availability of the weaponry or how to access its capabilities. Paul's prayer is that they will understand and apply the power God has already given them in Christ.

Second, Paul prayed, "That Christ may dwell in your hearts through faith." This statement does not imply that Christ did not already dwell in them, but Paul wanted their awareness of Christ's presence to be an ever-present reality, not a temporary, emotion-driven experience. Faith assures us of the reality of Christ's continuing presence when the stirring of the emotions is a distant memory.

The awareness of the presence of the Spirit of Christ is a major motivator to both Christian witness and righteous living. Not only are we to live with the awareness of His power, but also with the awareness of His presence. Both of these conditions are the product of faith. Faith is, in the first instance, a gift of God, but faith can and must be strengthened by fervent prayer, frequent exposure to the word of God and continual Christian fellowship. This fellowship must be more than mere social interaction; it must be defined as meeting together for the purpose of mutual spiritual edification.

Third, Paul prayed, "That you, being rooted and grounded in love, may be able to comprehend with all the saints what is the width and length and depth and height — to know the love of Christ which passes knowledge." Paul wanted the Ephesians to get a complete understanding of the incredible love that Christ had for them.

The church at Ephesus faced trials and persecution. Things did not always go well with them. They certainly had every natural reason to be discouraged and to give up the battle. It is important to understand that trials are no indication of any lack of Christ's love for His church. In fact, a good case can be made for just the opposite. Paul wrote to the Romans that "The Spirit Himself bears witness with our spirit that we are children of God, and if children, then heirs — heirs of God and joint heirs with Christ — if indeed we suffer with Him, that we may also be glorified together" (Romans 8:16-17).

Trials and tribulations are not necessarily the wrath of God; they can merely be the result of our living in a sinful world. In this world, we are subject to the wrath of the devil, who goes about making every effort to destroy the faith and life of every believer. But we know from Romans 8:28 that "God is able to make all things work together for

CHAPTER 11

good to those who love Him and are the called according to His purpose." The love of God for us is shown in and through trials because the ultimate object of all these difficulties is to bring us into conformance with the image of His Son, Jesus. Every difficulty we face and respond to in faith brings us closer to that ultimate goal of true Christ-likeness.

The ability to comprehend the "love that passes knowledge" is an understanding that is acquired by faith. It is not an understanding that comes through the five natural senses, but is acquired only by supernatural Spirit-to-spirit communication.

Last, Paul prayed, "That the church would be filled with the fullness of God." The fullness of God is the likeness of Christ. Paul wrote to the Colossians, "It pleased the Father that in Him (Christ) should all the fullness dwell" (Colossians 1:19). And again in Colossians 2:9, he wrote, "In Him dwells all the fullness of the Godhead bodily." Jesus in His flesh experienced and exhibited the fullness of His Father, and we in whom Christ dwells can also experience the fullness of God. As followers of Christ, we will not demonstrate the fullness of God as fully as the Son of God did; however, God does desire to fill us to the greatest extent of our individual human capacity. Jesus was a perfect man, and He was the full expression of the "fullness of God" to humankind. Jesus was the earthly expression of the substance of God.

R. L. Brandt, in his book entitled *Praying with Paul*, wrote that Jesus was the fullest expression of God.

"He saw with the eyes of God; He heard with the ears of God; He spoke with the authority of God; He thought with the thoughts of God; He loved with the love of God; He moved with the plan of God; He knew with the knowledge of God; He acted with the will of God."

He was able to do all these things and act in this perfection because He was filled with God.

God wants to express Himself in like manner in the world today through disciples of Christ who are filled with the fullness of God. He can only do so to the extent we allow ourselves to be filled, and the ultimate measure of the degree to which we are filled with God is the extent to which we live in obedience to His will. We are to present our bodies as a living sacrifice to God. The extent to which we have died to our self-will is the extent to which the fullness of God can dwell in us.

Doxology

Paul ends this second prayer with a doxology. A doxology is a spontaneous outburst of praise. In this doxology, the focus is on the power of God that exceeds every thought and imagination of which our minds are capable. However, this power is not far away and inaccessible; it is actually present and at work in every believer. This is another reminder that the same power that raised Jesus from the dead now lives in the one who believes.

Paul's reference to the glory that the church brings to God is a theme to which he frequently returns. Paul firmly

CHAPTER 11

believed that the mercy of God revealed in the plan of
salvation is the crowning glory of God. The church, the
congregation of the redeemed, will exist for all eternity as
a monument to the grace of God. This condescension to
fallen man is a puzzle and amazement to all the heavenly
hosts. It is something the angels long to look into but
cannot understand. Paul's effusion of praise is a reflection
of the awe in which he held the revelation of God's plan.

CHAPTER 12
THE WORTHY WALK

Ephesians 4:1-6:

I therefore, the prisoner of the Lord, beseech you that ye walk worthy of the vocation wherewith ye are called, [2] With all lowliness and meekness, with longsuffering, forbearing one another in love; [3] Endeavouring to keep the unity of the Spirit in the bond of peace. [4] There is one body, and one Spirit, even as ye are called in one hope of your calling; [5] One Lord, one faith, one baptism, [6] One God and Father of all, who is above all, and through all, and in you all (KJV).

With these verses we begin the second part of the "Sit, Walk, Stand" outline introduced at the beginning of this study.

Paul began by calling on the Ephesians to "walk worthy of their calling." This section begins an explanation of how our position in Christ will influence how we conduct our lives.

The use of the word "therefore" causes us to recall all that has been said up to this point and understand that what is to follow flows out of what has gone before. All that has been written up to this point is the foundation and motivation for what Paul now prescribes as the mandatory Christian lifestyle.

Chapter 12

The first and foremost characteristic of the walk that arises out of our position in Christ is unity.

When this letter was written, the sectarianism and denominationalism which now divides the body of Christ had not yet arisen. However, the divisions between Jew and Gentile, slave and free, rich and poor, were issues that even the early church had to address. Paul, on more than one occasion, had to address the specter of the "party spirit."

While it may seem that the emphasis is on the elimination of "parties" in the local body, the solution to this problem ultimately lies with the individual Christian and his responsibility for maintaining peaceful and respectful relationships with fellow believers. Paul delineated the essentials for unity in the local body and declared that if they would keep these things at the forefront of their relationships, they would find the forces that bound them together were far stronger than the differences that might tend to tear them apart.

Walk in Unity

In verses 4 through 6, Paul called the Ephesians to unity, citing a series of "ones" which were fundamental to the existence of the church.

Paul emphasized that there is only one body: The church has only one Head, and that Head is Jesus Christ. While there may be many under-shepherds, there is only one Shepherd, and while there may be many "elders," there is only one "Bishop" of our souls.

There is only one Spirit: Believers are indwelt by one and the same Spirit, the Spirit of Christ, which bears witness with our spirits that we are now children of God.

There is only one hope: There is only One who raises us from the dead. There is only one destiny and eternal dwelling place for believers.

There is only one Lord: There is only one Savior; only one Builder of the church; only one Will to be obeyed.

There is only one faith: The Old Covenant under which the Jews had lived has now been superseded by the New Covenant which is a better covenant in the person of Jesus Christ. However, the New Covenant was built upon and was an extension of the Old Covenant. The New Covenant is a better covenant, but primarily in the sense that it was a fulfillment rather than a replacement for the old.

There is only one baptism: Believers are only baptized into Christ, and that is an action that is accomplished by the Holy Spirit. The person who performs a water baptism is of no significance at all. Water baptism is the outward testimony of the spiritual baptism into the body of Christ which the Holy Spirit has already accomplished.

While there is the baptism in the Holy Spirit, and it is subsequent to being baptized into the body of Christ, there is no conflict because Paul's purpose here is to suppress sectarianism in the early church based on the human agent responsible for the believer's conversion or based on who may have performed the physical act of water baptism.

Chapter 12

And, finally, there is only one God and Father of all. Ultimately, Paul boiled it down to the essence: There is only one God, only one Son and only one way to be saved. All must accept these truths, and these truths remove all reason for disunity.

Unifying Attitudes and Actions

For all these reasons, in God's eyes, there is unity between true followers of His Son, yet the sad fact is these same followers don't always act in unity. You may liken this to the situation in which the individual believer often finds himself. When a person believes in Jesus, has his sins forgiven and is baptized by the Holy Spirit into Christ, that person becomes heir to the righteousness of Christ and will never be more holy in God's eyes than he is at that moment. However, despite the position of holiness he has been granted, he doesn't always act in consonance with that position.

Likewise, in God's eyes, all believers are united in Christ. However, the spiritual realities of personal holiness and unity must be worked out in the natural world. This is a process the Holy Spirit initiates in believers to make the spiritual position they have been granted in Christ visible in the outflow of their lives.

In this passage, Paul lists a number of actions and attitudes that must be developed if unity is to be more than a vague spiritual concept. These characteristics included lowliness, gentleness (meekness), longsuffering and bearing with one another.

Lowliness

First, in order to display unity in the church, every member must practice lowliness. Lowliness requires that one have a realistic view of himself. Lowliness is not self-loathing, but coming to understand that to have the mind of Christ one must have a servant heart. Lowliness carries the connotation of humility and modesty. Paul, in Romans 12:3, gives a good definition of lowliness. "For I say, through the grace given to me, to everyone who is among you, not to think of himself more highly than he ought to think, but to think soberly, as God has dealt to each one a measure of faith."

The concept of lowliness becomes even clearer when Philippians 2:3-4 is taken into consideration. "Let nothing be done through selfish ambition or conceit, but in lowliness of mind let each esteem others better than himself. ⁴Let each of you look out not only for his own interests, but also for the interests of others."

A person who practices lowliness suppresses the prideful attitudes that result in conflict and disunity.

Gentleness or Meekness

Second, unity is dependent on the practice of gentleness. In this case, "gentleness" is synonymous with "meekness." Neither of these concepts ever carries the connotation of weakness.

The Bible says that Moses was the meekest man that ever lived. Jesus, of course, has dethroned Moses from that position, but both Moses and Jesus stand as supreme

Chapter 12

examples of strength, power and authority.

Meekness is best understood as power under restraint. It has been compared to the horse which submits itself to the bridle, harness and the will of its handler. The practice of gentleness or meekness means to refuse to use one's power to wound, injure or demonstrate superiority, particularly in response to an injury or offense. Meekness turns the other cheek because it is the right thing to do, not because of fear of taking any other action.

For example, picture the heavyweight champion fighter taking abuse from the proverbial 90-pound weakling. Although he could destroy the smaller man, meekness restrains his response. The meek person uses his strength to control his actions rather than to retaliate or humiliate another. Meekness sacrifices itself for the benefit of another.

Longsuffering

Third, the maintenance of unity requires longsuffering. Longsuffering is patience extended and raised to a higher level. Longsuffering enables endurance in the face of adversity, trial and personal abuse. Longsuffering forgives not just once or seven times or even 70 times seven. Longsuffering endures adversity without retaliation as long as the offense continues. Longsuffering means delaying indefinitely any vengeful or retaliatory actions.

Longsuffering also has a sense of "turning the other cheek." It has the connotation of willingly accepting, indeed, almost permitting, continuation of offenses, if love and the Spirit of God demands it.

Jesus is our example of longsuffering. He allowed Himself to be beaten, mocked, spit upon and ultimately crucified when He had it in His power to stop it. He chose to allow the torture to continue because He knew what God was accomplishing through His suffering.

Longsuffering is something we freely choose. It can never be imposed upon us without our consent, as we respond to the leading of the Spirit.

Bearing With One Another

The fourth characteristic that is necessary for Christian unity is "bearing with one another in love." Walking in unity means that we put up with one another. The world's philosophy is "I don't have to put up with your garbage." The clear message of our society is that we have the right to be free from pain, problems and inconveniences, especially those that are deliberately imposed by other people. As a result, many tend to act as if they have the right to expect everyone to conform themselves to their needs and expectations. This philosophy flies directly in the face of scriptural principle of "bearing with one another in love."

Now, lest we conclude that Christians have no recourse but to accept continual abuse, it must be understood that none of the characteristics that are necessary for unity exclude the possibility and, indeed, the demand for rebuke, admonition and discipline to be administered out of concern for the offender's spiritual wellbeing. The object of these actions is to bring the offender to repentance and restoration.

When we experience an action that offends, we automatically assume the offense was deliberate, but if we speak to the offender in meekness and love, we may find the offense was unintentional, and the strain on the relationship will be immediately relieved.

The final truth that Paul revealed in this passage is that unity is not automatic; it does not always flow spontaneously out of human nature, even from those who by faith in Christ have been given a new nature. In regard to our efforts to live in unity, Paul used the word "endeavor." "Endeavor" means to diligently exert effort in the pursuit of a goal. In other words, maintaining unity requires a lot of hard work. The word "endeavor" also carries the implication of "speediness" or "promptness." The preservation of unity means that our response to offenses must be proper and prompt.

Regardless of our efforts, the word "endeavor" does not imply that we will always be successful. Our attempts to preserve unity may sometimes fail, despite our consistent loving efforts. We are not mandated to succeed, but to try.

When our efforts fail, we can look to Romans 12:17-18 for our direction. "Repay no one evil for evil. Have regard for good things in the sight of all men. If it is possible, as much as depends on you, live peaceably with all men. Beloved, do not avenge yourselves, but rather give place to wrath; for it is written, 'Vengeance is Mine, I will repay,' says the Lord. Therefore, if your enemy is hungry, feed him; If he is thirsty, give him a drink; For in so doing you will heap coals of fire on his head. Do not be overcome by evil, but overcome evil with good."

The key words here are "if possible, as much as depends on you." Therefore, Paul's admonition can be restated this way: "Let it never be said that unity was dissolved because of your actions or lack of action."

Every believer has a personal responsibility for the preservation of unity in the body of Christ. When unity is disrupted, believers are mandated to take responsibility and do everything within their power to affect restoration. However, we must remember that only as the offenders, together with the offended, follow the leading of the Spirit can true unity be restored and maintained.

CHAPTER 13
GIFTS FOR EQUIPPING

Ephesians 4:7-16:

But unto every one of us is given grace according to the measure of the gift of Christ. ⁸Wherefore he saith, When he ascended up on high, he led captivity captive, and gave gifts unto men. ⁹(Now that he ascended, what is it but that he also descended first into the lower parts of the earth? ¹⁰He that descended is the same also that ascended up far above all heavens, that he might fill all things.) ¹¹And he gave some, apostles; and some, prophets; and some, evangelists; and some, pastors and teachers; ¹²For the perfecting of the saints, for the work of the ministry, for the edifying of the body of Christ: ¹³Till we all come in the unity of the faith, and of the knowledge of the Son of God, unto a perfect man, unto the measure of the stature of the fulness of Christ: ¹⁴That we henceforth be no more children, tossed to and fro, and carried about with every wind of doctrine, by the sleight of men, and cunning craftiness, whereby they lie in wait to deceive; ¹⁵But speaking the truth in love, may grow up into him in all things, which is the head, even Christ: ¹⁶From whom the whole body fitly joined together and compacted by that which every joint supplieth, according to the effectual working in the measure of every part, maketh increase of the body unto the edifying of itself in love (KJV).

There is biblical evidence to suggest that in Old Testament times, and even in New Testament times, the daughters of the wealthy were given servants to help them prepare for their upcoming weddings. We find our best Old Testament example in the story of Rebekah's marriage to Isaac. When Isaac was of marriageable age, Abraham sent his servant Eliezer back to his former home in Mesopotamia to seek a bride for his son. Abraham's brother, Nahor, had remained there, and it was from his family that he hoped to procure a wife for Isaac.

Upon his arrival in Mesopotamia, God enables Eliezer to quickly identify a potential bride for Isaac. One of the first people he met was Rebekah, the granddaughter of Nahor and the sister of Laban, who was at that time the head of the family. After some negotiation with Laban, Rebekah was released to go with Eliezer to become Isaac's wife. Eliezer gave many gifts of gold and silver jewelry and fine clothes to the prospective bride. As the bridal party left Laban's house, Rebekah was given a number of maids to accompany her, to serve her and help her prepare for her wedding.

This story contains many of what theologians would call "types and shadows," representing things yet to come. The story reflects the story of the bride of Christ.

Abraham can be seen to be a type of God the Father, and Isaac is a foreshadowing of Jesus, the Son of God. Eliezer represents the Holy Spirit who has been sent into the world to call the bride and give her gifts. Rebekah represents the church, the bride of Christ. Eliezer's gifts to her represent the gifts the Holy Spirit gives to the church.

Rebekah's maidservants, therefore, must represent those who are called by God to help prepare the bride of Christ for the wedding with the Lamb. The maidservants in this analogy then represent the apostles, prophets, evangelists, pastors and teachers who are sent to build up the church "till we all come to the unity of the faith and of the knowledge of the Son of God, to a perfect man, to the measure of the stature of the fullness of Christ."

The Holy Spirit, His gifts and those called to special ministry to the bride of Christ are all important to the accomplishment of the purpose of Paul's Letter to the Ephesians. His purpose is to bring them to a "walk worthy of the calling to which you were called," which is to walk in peace and unity.

The Gifts of God

To enable believers to "walk worthy of their calling," God has given to each member of the bride of Christ a measure of grace. Thayer's Greek Dictionary defines grace as "the kindness of God manifested in His divine influence on the lives of believers, exhibiting His holy influence on their souls, turning them to Christ, keeping, strengthening and increasing them in Christian faith, knowledge and affection, and kindling in them the exercise of all Christian virtues." A simple definition that covers all these aspects and more is "Grace is God working on the believer's behalf." Of course, His ultimate goal for every believer is to create within them the image of Christ.

The extent of this grace is defined by the magnitude of the sacrifice Christ made for us. We recognize the sacrifice He made by His incarnation as a human being and His subsequent physical suffering and death. Yet the greatest measure of His sacrifice is perhaps none of these, but the agony of separation from the Father He suffered as a result of His taking upon Himself the sins of us all.

The Role of the Servant Gifts

Just like Eliezer gave gifts to Rebekah, the Holy Spirit has given gifts to the bride of Christ. These gifts are manifestations of the grace of God. Just as Rebekah needed maidservants to properly use and adorn herself with the gifts Eliezer had given her, the bride of Christ also needs servants to help her understand how she is to use the gifts that God has given her.

God has given servant leaders to His Son's bride to help her adorn herself and get the most benefit from the gifts of God's grace. Paul lists five different types of servant leaders: apostles, prophets, evangelists, pastors and teachers.

Apostles

Apostles (the sent-out ones) are those commissioned to go out to preach the gospel in new areas with miraculous signs confirming the word. Another apostolic role was to establish local churches and local leadership and oversee their spiritual health. Although this could be a reference to the original 12, the New Testament makes several references to certain others as apostles who were not part of the original 12.

In the church of today, the gifting of apostle seems to be most visible in those we call missionaries, particularly those who are called to regions where the gospel has never been preached. In areas where the church is well-established, apostolic gifts are also manifested in those who provide broad-based leadership and spiritual oversight.

Prophets

Prophets declare the plans and purposes of God. The Old Testament prophets were frequently used by God to remind the people of His previously revealed will, purposes and commands. Prophets were also used by God to reveal future events, such as famines, notable births, national victories and defeats. The most significant Old Testament prophesies involved the coming of the Messiah. Although prophets, at times, gave purely predictive messages, most often the predictive elements of their message were to reveal the consequences of continued disobedience to the known will of God.

The New Testament prophet should be expected to carry the same mantle as their Old Testament predecessors. Their role must include warnings to the church and individual believers and reminding the church of God's previously revealed purposes. The predictions of the New Testament prophet will involve consequences of continued disobedience, as well as foretelling of future events, especially when the church has a special need to prepare for the event.

Evangelists

In the church of today, the office of evangelists is perhaps the most enigmatic of the ministry gifts. An evangelist is the "bringer of good news," but the Scriptures do not clearly define the specific arena of their service. Timothy was a pastor, but he was admonished to do the work of an evangelist. Apostles, as they went into new areas preaching the gospel, must certainly have been "bringers of good news." Consequently, the work of the evangelism does not seem to have been the exclusive purview of the "evangelist."

Perhaps evangelists can be best defined as "preachers of the gospel," but they were not identified as necessarily being workers of miracles, nor do we see that they had ongoing leadership or supervisory responsibilities. Perhaps their specific role can be identified as those who preach in areas where the church has already been established. Evangelists might be thought of as the "second wave" of preachers following the apostle's establishment of the church in a new area. Since all these offices have the responsibility for "equipping the saints for the work of the ministry," their role could also involve training and admonishing the existing body of Christ to be effective in its work of evangelism.

Chapter 13

Pastors

"Pastor" is from the Greek word for shepherd. It pictures the overseer of a local assembly of believers. Looking at the duties of a Middle Eastern shepherd from Bible times, we get an idea of the role a pastor is to play.

The shepherd's duties included finding food and water for his flock. The shepherd played an essential role in the care of domesticated sheep. They could not find their own food and water, therefore, they had to be led to it. Without the shepherd, the domestic sheep would starve. The shepherd was constantly on guard against those animals which would prey on the relatively helpless sheep. His role was to protect them with his own life, if necessary.

The shepherd was also expected to look after the health of his sheep. He tended their wounds and ministered to their diseases. The shepherd was also responsible for rescuing those who fell into areas from which they could not escape and for retrieving those that got separated from the flock.

The shepherd loved his sheep in the "agape" sense. He dedicated himself to the flock's wellbeing, often at the expense of his own safety, convenience or comfort.

Christian pastors will find themselves faced with these same privileges and responsibilities. They will feed the flock from the word of God, warn against sin and false teachers and be proactive in seeking out those who have wandered away and become lost to the flock.

Of course, Jesus was the Good Shepherd, and He is the ultimate role model for the local pastor.

Teachers

There are those who consider the role of teacher to be included in the role of the pastor. In other words, there are really only four ministry gifts, the fourth being "pastor-teacher." In defense of this notion, it is certainly true that the pastor has a significant role as a teacher in the church under his care.

However, as a separate ministry gift, the teacher would be one in the Christian assembly whom the Holy Spirit has specifically anointed with a supernatural ability to instruct others with gentleness and clarity.

The Epistle of James warns that one is not to take the role of teacher lightly, because there is a sterner judgment on those who instruct others, yet do not live up to the standards they teach.

Blending of Roles

It becomes obvious to even the casual observer that these servant leaders may at times operate in a variety of these roles or in combinations of these roles. For example, a pastor will certainly operate as a teacher or, as was true of Timothy, as an evangelist. However, the pastor will retain as his primary love the care and feeding of a local church body.

An evangelist may slip into an apostolic mode or may serve as a pastor, but the evangelist will have as his first priority the preaching of the "Good News" to the lost.

An apostle will always have the desire to "boldly go where no man has gone before" to establish a new outpost

CHAPTER 13

of the church of Jesus Christ, but he will also find himself in the role of evangelist and perhaps, from time to time, in the role of pastor.

The Purpose of the Servant Leader

The servant leaders' job is to equip the saints for the work of the ministry. The work of the ministry, in simple terms, is preaching the gospel to the lost and building up believers so that the new believers can, in turn, preach the gospel to the lost.

We have already established that the servant leaders are given by Christ to His bride to help her fully operate in the grace God has imparted to her. Paul uses two words to define this work: edify and equip.

Although Paul places "edify" after "equip" in his letter, let's first consider what it means to edify the body of Christ. The result of edification will be an increase in the ability to yield to the grace of God and to allow that holy influence to bring about the changes God desires. A further result of edification is the increase of the church's knowledge of God, both educationally and experientially. Edification also has the effect of strengthening our faith and solidifying our ability to trust God in all circumstances.

In the definition of the various special roles of the five-fold ministry gifts, we have, in general, defined the mission of the church. However, we now see the real purpose of the servant leaders is not to only *do* the work of the ministry, but to *equip* the saints, to give the saints the tools and motivation that will enable them to do what Christ has ordained them to do. So, therefore, the final result of edification *is* equipping.

While the pastor of a local church may have the primary responsibility of protecting, defending and providing for the spiritual needs of the local body, no one person can do all the pastoring even a small group of people will require.

Pastors must make their first priority the equipping of the body to protect, defend and feed itself. That's what is meant by "equipping the body for the work of the ministry."

In their own particular sphere, the other ministry gifts have the same duality of purpose: to go, to prophesy, to preach, to teach, but also to train and prepare the body to do those works as well.

How Long Will These Ministry Gifts be Needed?

Paul envisions that these gifts will continue to be present and needed in the church until Jesus comes again and the saints are changed in the twinkling of an eye into the perfect expression of the image of Jesus.

These ministry gifts will continue to function:

- Until we come to the unity of the faith.
- Until we have fully developed the image of Christ.
- Until we can no longer be deceived by false teachers.
- Until love of Christ is our single motivation.

Chapter 13

- Until the body works effectively, recognizing and appreciating the essential role each member plays in the maturing of the whole.

Since the church, as a whole, has not reached this ideal state, nor is it ever likely to, apostles, prophets, evangelists, pastors and teachers will continue to be called and anointed and will remain fully employed until the coming of the Lord Jesus Christ.

God is moving us toward our ultimate destination in Him, and that destination is the perfection of the image of Christ in the individual and the corporate body. Jeremiah 29:11 reads, "'I know the plans I have for you,' says the Lord, 'plans for good and not for evil, to give you a hope and a future.'" God is good. God is love. God can do no evil, neither can He act in any way unloving. The one thing God cannot do is act contrary to His nature. He cannot deny Himself.

Paul tells us in Romans 8:29 that God has predestined all believers to be conformed to the image of His Son, Jesus. And the implication of Romans 8:28 is that everything that happens in the believer's life is intended to develop that image. So, "all things work together for good" because all things, when accepted as coming from a loving God, will bring about the intended result.

The goal of the grace of God (which is at work through the internal work of the Spirit of God and, externally, through the ministry of the apostles, prophets, evangelists, pastors and teachers) is to move us toward a predetermined destination. Paul describes that destination as "a perfect man, having the stature of Christ, mature in the knowledge of God and mature in our relationships with each other."

All believers, defined as true followers of Christ, are on their way to being spiritually mature, accurately reflecting the image of Christ. By the ministry of the Spirit, we experience God and come into a fuller knowledge of His nature, character and will. The more we experience God and the more we are conformed to His image by that knowledge, the better our relationship with other believers will become. What has been said of the marriage relationship is also true of all Christian interactions. The closer to God we come, the closer we will be to each other. The more like Christ we each become, the less will be the opportunities for conflict.

God's desired destination for us is that we achieve harmonious working relationships with every other member of the body of Christ. We are on our way, but we have not reached our destination, therefore, the Spirit will continue to work in us and use those ministry gifts to keep us moving toward our goal.

CHAPTER 14
MOVING TOWARD MATURITY

Ephesians 4:17-32:

This I say therefore, and testify in the Lord, that ye henceforth walk not as other Gentiles walk, in the vanity of their mind, [18] Having the understanding darkened, being alienated from the life of God through the ignorance that is in them, because of the blindness of their heart: [19] Who being past feeling have given themselves over unto lasciviousness, to work all uncleanness with greediness. [20] But ye have not so learned Christ; [21] If so be that ye have heard him, and have been taught by him, as the truth is in Jesus: [22] That ye put off concerning the former conversation the old man, which is corrupt according to the deceitful lusts; [23] And be renewed in the spirit of your mind; [24] And that ye put on the new man, which after God is created in righteousness and true holiness. [25] Wherefore putting away lying, speak every man truth with his neighbour: for we are members one of another. [26] Be ye angry, and sin not: let not the sun go down upon your wrath: [27] Neither give place to the devil. [28] Let him that stole steal no more: but rather let him labour, working with his hands the thing which is good, that he may have to give to him that needeth. [29] Let no corrupt communication proceed out of your mouth, but that which is good to the use of edifying, that it may minister grace unto the hearers. [30] And grieve not the Holy Spirit of God, whereby ye are sealed unto the day of redemption. [31] Let all bitterness, and wrath, and anger, and clamour, and evil speaking, be put away from you, with all malice: [32] And be ye kind one to another, tenderhearted, forgiving one another, even as God for Christ's sake hath forgiven you (KJV).

You Are Not Where You Once Were

Even as we realize we are not yet at our ultimate destination, we also realize we are not where we once were. Paul's description of the Gentile's former condition is reflective of a past life all believers share to a greater or lesser extent.

We once walked in the futility (spiritual helplessness) of our own minds. We once depended upon our own spiritual understanding, which means that we once had no spiritual understanding and no capability to understand, because "spiritual things are spiritually discerned."

We once were alienated from God. We walked in willful ignorance. The knowledge of Himself that God had made evident to all mankind had been rejected. We deliberately chose to ignore the evidences of our own senses. Even to the natural mind there are many evidences that point to the existence of God, but it suited our purposes to pretend ignorance of them.

Our hearts were once afflicted with blindness. This word "blindness" could be translated "hardness," which implies no feelings, no conscience, no sensitivity to the conviction by the Holy Spirit. Where there is spiritual life, there is feeling. Where there is no life, there is numbness, no feeling, no quickening.

We were once pleasure-driven and without conscience. We were "past feeling," having lost the natural awareness of God and His requirements for human behavior. Our innate sense of right and wrong had been seared over.

We were given over to seeking the pleasures of the flesh and ready to participate in every kind of self-indulgence with passion and fervor.

At the worst, we were "given over to lewdness, to work all uncleanness with greediness." This means we once pursued sin as one would pursue a business. We worked at sinning. We sought every kind of sin by all available means. This condition is very common in our present world.

The Path to Change

Getting from where we were, utterly spiritually dead in trespasses and sin, to where we now find ourselves, beginning to display the image of Christ by the transforming power of the Holy Spirit, obviously involves a process. However, this process cannot begin until one is born again and receives a new nature that is capable of knowing and obeying God. Our old nature has no such capability.

The means by which believers get from "where you were" to "where you are going" is a process of deliberately "putting off" certain behaviors and "putting on" certain others. Believers, because they have been given a "new nature," now by the power of the indwelling Holy Spirit have the ability to alter their behavior and conform to the nature and character of Christ.

What to Put Off

The list of behaviors to be "put off," although extensive, is not all-inclusive. Paul does not intend this list to become a catalogue for "performance-based holiness," but a reminder of all the things that can be eliminated from the believer's life as he continues to walk in obedience to the Spirit. He says we are to "put off" or stop doing these things because we are now spiritually capable of doing so. Putting off the old man involves the renewing of the mind. Renewing the mind is accomplished by letting God take control of the mind every day. It is something that is already done, but is never fully complete. It is not something we can do for ourselves, but something we allow God to do in us. The mind that is being renewed will begin and continue to exhibit increasing levels of true righteousness and holiness. With the renewed mind, we will see the following things accomplished:

We can stop lying.

We can stop nursing our anger and rid ourselves of it quickly.

We can stop exposing ourselves to temptation by avoiding places and situations where evil's power would be most intense.

Chapter 14

We can stop stealing.

We can stop being lazy and do honorable work.

(Here we have a great explanation of the right motive for Christians to work and earn even more than is necessary for personal needs or for the survival needs of those dependent on them. Giving in the early church was almost always focused on supporting itinerant, God-called ministers or on giving alms to supply the necessities of life to the poor. Contrary to today's situation, in the early days of the church, there was no significant local paid clergy and practically no church-owned buildings to be maintained.)

We can stop being a "garbage mouth." Corrupt communication means decayed and rotten and is used to describe spoiled meat and rotten fruit. This refers to any speech that dishonors God or man or speaks favorably or lightly of sin and perverted behaviors.

We can be rid of bitterness, which comes from unresolved anger and leads to hatred.

We can be rid of wrath, those sudden fits of rage, which almost always lead to physical or verbal abuse.

We can be free of the anger which promotes the taking of revenge.

We can be rid of a quarrelsome nature, which almost always comes from a prideful spirit.

We can put away "evil speaking," which involves slandering people and blaspheming God. In other words, the Christian controls his tongue. He avoids speaking evil and instead concentrates on speaking "those things that make for peace, and things wherewith we may edify one another" (1 Corinthians 8:1).

The things we are to eliminate from our lives are all things that do not reflect the image of Christ. The Holy Spirit, Who indwells the believer, will promote and enable the cessation of any behaviors which do not reflect or honor the likeness of Christ. In allowing the Holy Spirit to remove these things from our lives, we reduce or eliminate the risk of grieving the Holy Spirit.

What to Put On

As the Bible often illustrates, there is no such thing as a spiritual vacuum. The works of the flesh must be replaced by the fruit of the Spirit. If there are actions and attitudes of the flesh to be put off, then there must be actions and attitudes of the Spirit to be "put on." These behaviors to be "put on" are Spirit-enabled abilities which naturally (really, supernaturally) flow out of the new nature and the new creation the believer has become in Christ. Again, Paul's list of things to be put on is not intended to be exhaustive, but representative.

Put on a healthy work ethic. Instead of stealing, the believer must learn to work and appreciate the values and purpose of work. Work must not be seen as a means to satisfy the selfish desires of our own flesh, but as a means to meet our needs, promote the kingdom of God and, as a practical expression of our love of God, assist in meeting the needs of others. Put succinctly, "Stop stealing, and start giving."

CHAPTER 14

Put on kindness. Be pleasant. Be someone other people, whether believers or non-believers, enjoy being around. Be agreeable, not combative. Be benevolent. This certainly means to be generous in a material sense, but to also be generous in your attitude toward others and their faults and foibles. This means Christians are to have a generosity of spirit.

Put on tenderheartedness. The Spirit enables the believer to be compassionate, to share grief and sorrow at a level far deeper than a mere verbal expression of concern.

Put on forgiveness. We have little capability to control our emotional reactions. However, we do have the ability, especially when enabled by the Holy Spirit, to control our actions. Forgiveness, as a practical matter, has little to do with feeling. Forgiveness is not about eliminating the emotions of hurt, anger and disappointment which follow an injury, but about controlling our actions. To forgive means we make a deliberate decision to refuse to retaliate in any way against the one who has hurt us. We choose to forego punishing the offender or vindicating ourselves.

When we fail to put off the wrong actions and put on the right actions, we grieve the Spirit. This literally means to cause the Spirit to experience sadness, sorrow and emotional pain. When we read this, we tend to think the Spirit's reaction to His hurt will be expressed in human terms: anger, retribution and withdrawal. However, Paul does not attribute these reactions to the Spirit in retaliation for our offensive behavior. Perhaps the point to be taken here is that when we know we are hurting someone we love, that knowledge motivates and demands a change in behavior. Jesus spoke to this most clearly, "If you love Me, you will keep My commandments." He also said, "A new commandment I give to you, that you love one another." So, therefore, when we fail to love one another by continually and actively promoting each other's welfare, we grieve the Holy Spirit. The only practical way to express our love of God is by loving other people.

How is This Change Affected?

Even when we know what we were and have an understanding of what we are to become, the question still remains: "How do those changes actually happen?" The answer is both simple and profound: Only by the grace of God! The grace of God has already been defined as "God at work on your behalf." The Scriptures say that God is at work in us "both to will and to do of His good pleasure," meaning that God gives us both the desire to follow the leading of the Spirit and the ability to do so.

The grace of God doesn't excuse sin, but the grace of God does free us from the ruling power of sin. We *choose* righteousness by His strength, and we *walk* in righteousness by His strength.

Because of the grace of God, we no longer have to sin, although we may still do so from time to time. When we do sin, we put on the "old man" rather than the "new man." The "old nature" gains ascendency at the moment our desire to gratify the flesh is stronger than our desire to please God. When writing to the Galatians, Paul said, "Walk in the Spirit and you will not fulfill the desires of the flesh" (Galatians 5:16).

In other words, you always walk in one or the other. We either walk in the flesh or we walk in the Spirit; we cannot walk in both at the same time. Christian maturity and sanctification occurs as we do the will of God as opposed to doing what the flesh would want.

The process works something like this: We are faced with a choice of pleasing God or taking an action that will gratify the opposing desires of the flesh. Remember, we are no longer obligated to follow the desires of our flesh, because the Spirit of God now lives in us to enable us to act in accordance with the righteous new nature, rather than the sin-plagued old nature.

In a moment of weakness, we may choose to gratify the flesh rather than follow the leading of the Spirit. The Spirit is grieved by this action, but He does not depart, but rather begins to call our attention to His grief by what we call conviction. If we are spiritually mature, we stop the process right there. We immediately confess our sin, repent, correct our behavior and make proper restitution as necessary.

If we are not spiritually mature, we justify ourselves and persist in our offensive behavior. At that point, God begins the process of chastisement. He will bring negative circumstances into our lives to help us understand we have no justification for our sin and to make the pain of our estrangement from Him so acute that our desire to please Him and be restored to fellowship becomes greater than our desire to continue to please our flesh. In other words, our spiritual pain begins to outweigh our fleshly pleasure, and we come to desire the restoration of relationship that comes only through a return to obedience.

This is the typical pattern of spiritual growth and maturity: obeying, disobeying, being convicted and chastised, repenting, being restored and always moving toward a time of spiritual perfection in which our first and only impulse is to obey God.

Chapter 15
Walk in Love

Ephesians 5:1-7:

Be ye therefore followers of God, as dear children;
²And walk in love, as Christ also hath loved us, and hath
given himself for us an offering and a sacrifice to God for a
sweetsmelling savour. ³But fornication, and all
uncleanness, or covetousness, let it not be once named
among you, as becometh saints; ⁴Neither filthiness, nor
foolish talking, nor jesting, which are not convenient: but
rather giving of thanks. ⁵For this ye know, that no
whoremonger, nor unclean person, nor covetous man,
who is an idolater, hath any inheritance in the kingdom of
Christ and of God. ⁶Let no man deceive you with vain
words: for because of these things cometh the wrath of
God upon the children of disobedience. ⁷Be not ye
therefore partakers with them (KJV).

In chapter 5, Paul continues his discussion of the Christian "Walk." In chapter 4, the emphasis was on "walking worthy of the calling with which you were called." Chapter 4's challenge included walking in unity, walking in the Spirit and to walk away from all the sins of the flesh which characterized the lifestyles of the unbelieving Gentiles. The emphasis in chapter 5 is walking in love, which, in a way, serves to summarize all the previous challenges to walk worthy of the One Who has called us. To walk in love means to imitate God's loving nature in all our relationships with believers and non-believers.

Be Imitators of God

Several years ago, a clever ad in a national anti-smoking campaign depicted a young father with his preschool-aged son sitting close to him under a tree in a beautiful meadow. The father seemed to be absorbed in the beauty around him as he lit a cigarette and inhaled deeply. As he exhaled, he put the cigarette package and lighter on the ground between himself and his son.

Immediately, the little boy picked up the cigarettes and lighter and emulated his father's every action in an attempt to smoke.

The point is that when we love and respect someone, we will be highly motivated to improve ourselves by imitating him or her. The ones we love exert a tremendous influence on our behavior. Therefore, if we love God, as His children, we will begin to emulate His attitudes and actions.

In attempting to explain human behavior, the argument regarding the relative effects of nature (genetics) and nurture (environment) continues. It is not proven that children inherit from their parents the predisposition toward certain behaviors.

However, while the debate regarding natural human behavior remains unresolved, the Scriptures make it clear

CHAPTER 15

that God, through the new birth, makes us partakers of the divine nature (1 Peter 5:1), and this divine nature makes itself evident. Therefore, imitators of God will, of necessity, reflect the nature and character of God in every aspect of their lives. We not only have God's example to follow, we also have His divine nature from which His likeness will flow.

Be a Good Imitation

When we think of imitations, we usually think of "knock-offs," which when compared to the originals are cheap, fake, phony and generally inferior in quality. The Greek word, which is translated "imitator," is the same word from which we get the English words "mime" and "mimic." All these words seem to give us the impression of something not to be compared favorably with the original. However, this is definitely not the impression Paul intended that we should give as "imitators of God."

We are not imitations of God, nor are we replicas of God, but we are always in the process of taking on the moral qualities of God. Unfortunately, we continue to present a mixture of godly and ungodly behaviors. When we do present godly behaviors and attitudes, they are real and are produced by the Holy Spirit in us, but the godly effect is offset by the continued presence of our flesh.

If you can imagine such a thing, we are being transformed from a Geo Metro into a Rolls Royce. We may have a Rolls steering wheel and Rolls taillights, while we still retain a lot of Geo-ness. We are being transformed, the process is continuing and the process will continue as long as we live. Little by little, the Geo parts are being replaced by the Rolls Royce parts. When we arrive in heaven, we will be glorified, and the process of becoming like Christ will be complete. "We will be like Him for we will see Him as He is" (1 John 3:2).

However, in terms of our ability to live in holiness, we are always going to be the Geo Metro to God's Rolls Royce. These two vehicles perform exactly the same basic function, the transportation of people from one place to another. However, the quality is much different. The Geo Metro and the Rolls Royce both represent the same class of machinery, the automobile, but one is Automotive Perfection, while the other has a long way to go. Jesus is the Perfection of the image of God. We, on the other hand, have a long way to go.

Imitate (Replicate) God's Love

We imitate God by walking in love, and the word translated here as "love" is the Greek word "agape."

"Agape," one of four Greek words for love, existed in the Greek lexicon long before the advent of Christ, but "agape" took on special meaning for followers of Christ and became the defining word of Christian behavior. The Greeks used "eros" to refer to physical or sexual love, and "phileo" to refer to "brotherly love," or the love between close friends. They also used the word "storge" to refer to the love between family members.

"Agape" is the only love word that does not necessarily

have an emotional motivational component. It is a love expressed in acts of service that arise from a commitment to the wellbeing of another. God loves us, therefore, He is committed to our eternal wellbeing. He loves (agape) by deliberate choice based on our need, not our merit. God's love has no cause except that which exists in the very nature of God. God's love is the kindness of God, meeting the needs of man, without regard for or despite the total lack of any worthiness in man.

"Agape" is love in action, action based on need, not on merit, worth or deservedness.

We are to be imitators of God in this practice of need-based love. For the rest of this chapter, when the word "love" is used, the reference will be to "agape."

Just as Christ loved us and gave Himself for us, we are also to love and give ourselves to the promoting of the wellbeing of others, both spiritually and materially.

The Antithesis of Love

Love always edifies; love always builds up its object. Paul refines our understanding of what love is by giving us a list of a number of actions that are not compatible with true love. These listed actions are all fleshly and self-serving.

Fornication (porniea): This includes sexual sin of all kinds. This is the only sin that is said to be "against one's self."

Uncleanness: Uncleanness also has a sexual connotation. It can be defined as lustful, profligate living and a selfish striving to fulfill every desire of the flesh. It includes all unnatural lusts such as homosexuality, lesbianism, child molestation and bestiality.

Covetousness: We think of covetousness as greediness, but the dictionary defines it as "to long to possess, especially what belongs to another; to desire unreasonably or unlawfully; to desire strongly; avaricious for gain." In the New Testament, covetousness is equated to idolatry or the worship of a god other than the true God.

Filthiness: This is obscene, shameful behavior that might not be included in the previously condemned behaviors.

Foolish talking: This term comes from the same root as the word "moron." This would include speaking contrary to the truth of God's word, especially when such speech comes out of a willful blindness. This describes empty conversations which are unfruitful in any way, especially spiritually. Foolish talking also includes ridiculing and exposing one another to contempt.

Coarse jesting: This would be any speech that would disparage, debase or dishonor others and make them the butt of a joke. This jesting is not joking, but the cunning use of words to deceive, including the deceptive use of words with double meaning (double entendre). It also includes indecent, off-color, sexually-based potty humor.

Don't be deceived. These anti-love behaviors do not come from the nature of God. Those who practice these things will suffer the wrath of God. In fact, in Galatians 5, Paul, after posting a similar list of the works of the flesh,

CHAPTER 15

flatly states, "Those who practice such things will not inherit the kingdom of God."

Loving, in the "agape" sense, is not an option for those who would "walk worthy of the calling with which you were called." For God's children, refusing to love is not an option. The incontrovertible truth is: If God dwells in you by His Spirit, He will become manifest in you. It is inevitable, for God has predestined you to become conformed to the image of His Son. The Christian who is indwelt by the Spirit of God will continue to produce the fruit of the Spirit. Paul lists the fruit of the Spirit in Galatians 5:22 as love, joy, peace, longsuffering, kindness, goodness, faithfulness, gentleness, self-control. Taken as a whole, this fruit of the Spirit is a representation of the likeness of Christ, which is to be manifest in every believer.

CHAPTER 16
WALK IN THE LIGHT

Ephesians 5:8-14:

For ye were sometimes darkness, but now are ye light in the Lord: walk as children of light: ⁹(For the fruit of the Spirit is in all goodness and righteousness and truth;) ¹⁰Proving what is acceptable unto the Lord. ¹¹And have no fellowship with the unfruitful works of darkness, but rather reprove them. ¹²For it is a shame even to speak of those things which are done of them in secret. ¹³But all things that are reproved are made manifest by the light: for whatsoever doth make manifest is light. ¹⁴Wherefore he saith, Awake thou that sleepest, and arise from the dead, and Christ shall give thee light (KJV).

In Christian terminology, "light" has a number of meanings. Jesus said, "I am the light of the world." James tell us that "Every good gift and every perfect gift is from above, and comes down from the Father of lights, with whom there is no variation or shadow of turning. Of His own will He brought us forth by the word of truth, that we might be a kind of first fruits of His creatures" (James 1:17-18). This statement, when taken in conjunction with Jesus' statement that "You (meaning His disciples) are the light of the world," confirms Jesus' own claim to be the "light of the world," as well as His assertion that all who

Chapter 16

would come to Him by faith and follow Him would continue to carry that light.

We also refer to the message of salvation as the "light of the gospel," and John tells us, "But if we walk in the light as He is in the light, we have fellowship with one another, and the blood of Jesus Christ His Son cleanses us from all sin" (1 John 1:7).

Paul equates "walking in the light" to demonstrating the fruit of the Spirit. The listing given here is abbreviated when compared to the fruit of the Spirit listed in Galatians 5:22-23.

However, neither list can be considered exhaustive, since all Spirit-enabled, God-like characteristics could be considered "fruit of the Spirit." Walking in the light can be defined as doing whatever is acceptable to the Lord.

The psalmist, David, wrote, "Your word is a lamp unto my feet and a light unto my path" (Psalm 119:105). For discovering and maintaining an understanding of the light in which God wants us to walk, there is no substitute for reading the word of God. I use the word "reading" deliberately, because surveys have revealed that less than 6 percent of those who call themselves Christians have read the entire Bible from Genesis to Revelation. An even more shocking discovery is that less than 10 percent of Christian ministers have read the entire Bible.

Many have read parts of the Bible, and many have made in-depth studies of certain subjects in the Bible. Someone has likened this situation to looking at a jigsaw puzzle. Christians, ministers and laymen alike have studied individual pieces of the puzzle, but never put the whole puzzle together to see the big picture. The big picture is important. Only by seeing the big picture can one understand the relationships of the individual pieces to the whole. Getting a firm grip on the "whole counsel of God's word" is essential to "walking in the light."

As we read the word of God, particularly if we do so prayerfully, the Holy Spirit will illuminate the word to us. It is in the light of this Spirit illumination that we are able to "walk as children of the light." It is in this way that we can "find out what is acceptable to the Lord."

An essential part of walking in the light is avoiding the darkness. We are to have no fellowship with the unfruitful works of darkness. In other words, we cannot compromise with sin.

Compromise can be active or passive. Passive compromise occurs when we fail to state clearly why participation in an activity is unacceptable to us. Christians have a responsibility to stand on their biblical principles and, as necessary, state clearly why they cannot participate in the proposed activity, rather than constructing some excuse.

Active compromise doesn't necessarily mean actively participating in the sinful activity. It can mean just talking about the vile deeds of those who walk in darkness, particularly if the conversation does not contain an element of disapproval and reproof.

Paul issues a stern warning against having anything to do with walking in the darkness, which he would consider

CHAPTER 16

to be equivalent to "walking in the flesh" to satisfy the lusts thereof. In fact, Paul stresses that as partakers of the light, we have a duty to not only avoid but also to expose works of darkness and demonstrate just how offensive such things are to our Lord.

To walk in the light is to do and associate ourselves only with those things that are acceptable to Christ, and avoid all association or compromise with anything that would not bring honor and glory to our King.

Compromise can creep into our lives in subtle ways, and Paul's warning, "Awake, you who sleep, arise from the dead, and Christ will give you light," is particularly important for today's Christians.

Those who are asleep are not aware of the encroaching darkness. Constant exposure to the sins of others tends to anesthetize us to it, rather than arousing us to anger against the corruption of our society. The entertainment media, which has such a large presence in even the most devoted Christian's lifestyle, is saturated with positive representations of sinful deeds, worldly attitudes and corrupt lifestyles. Christians are frequently entertained by watching people portray sinful behaviors. Sometimes, this sinful behavior is presented in such a way as to be hilarious, even to the believer. Consequently, we are no longer shocked by sin; we have been trained to accept it or at least our negative reaction to it has been severely blunted.

Unfortunately, it seems the distance between accepting sin in others and accepting it in our own lives is quite short. Satan lulls us to sleep so that the encroaching worldliness seems right or at least not a cause for alarm. He appears as an "angel of light" to deceive many. The deception of the enemy, with his counterfeit light, can only be exposed by the true light of the gospel of Jesus Christ.

CHAPTER 17
WALK IN WISDOM

Ephesians 5:15-20:

See then that ye walk circumspectly, not as fools, but as wise, [16]Redeeming the time, because the days are evil. [17]Wherefore be ye not unwise, but understanding what the will of the Lord is. [18]And be not drunk with wine, wherein is excess; but be filled with the Spirit; [19]Speaking to yourselves in psalms and hymns and spiritual songs, singing and making melody in your heart to the Lord; [20]Giving thanks always for all things unto God and the Father in the name of our Lord Jesus Christ; (KJV).

<u>Walk in Wisdom</u>

To walk circumspectly means that we are to exert every effort to keep on the right course spiritually. We are to redeem the time and use our time productively by applying ourselves to the purposes of the kingdom of God.

To walk wisely or circumspectly means we don't lose focus and squander our time and energy on things that are not edifying, either spiritually, physically or emotionally, for ourselves or for others. Walking in wisdom involves "seeking first the kingdom of God and His righteousness," which means keeping all aspects of our lives in balance in accordance with the will of God for us. In the pursuit of the "kingdom of God and His righteousness," there will always be time for personal pursuits, family life, employment, recreation and fulfilling our own personal ministry calling. If any one of these areas gets crowded out, our lives are not in balance, and we have ceased to walk circumspectly. Achieving this balance is a matter of constantly and prayerfully asking God for guidance, because the "urgent" may crowd out the "important," and the "good" may keep us from the "best."

Proverbs 9:10 reads, "The fear of the LORD is the beginning of wisdom, and the knowledge of the Holy One is understanding." Therefore, there is no walking in wisdom that does not begin with knowing God.

Walking in wisdom also involves being like "the sons of Issachar who had understanding of the times, to know what Israel ought to do" (1 Chronicles 12:32). Walking in wisdom means we are constantly aware that the days are evil, and because this is true, there is no time to risk getting enamored with its attractions. The foolish man allows himself to get entangled with the world, but the wise man diligently seeks to know and do the will of God.

Walking in wisdom means we do not allow ourselves to become intoxicated by the wine of the world, which is probably even more dangerous to the spiritual man than alcoholic intoxication. However, alcohol use and abuse is only one symptom of intoxication with the things of the world. To be intoxicated by the world is to come under its controlling influence, but to become intoxicated with the Spirit is to come under the control of the Spirit of God.

CHAPTER 17

<u>"Be Filled with the Spirit": A Pentecostal Perspective</u>

Before we can begin to understand the real import of this passage, we must first understand the phrase in verse 18, "Be filled with the Spirit." Pentecostals and non-Pentecostals hold widely differing views on the meaning of this phrase.

The paragraph quoted below is a succinct and fairly accurate representation of a typical non-Pentecostal interpretation of the phrase "Be filled with the Spirit."

"When we receive Christ as our Savior, we are immediately <u>indwelt</u> by the Holy Spirit. That can never be <u>changed</u>. But each moment, we must surrender control to the Holy Spirit. That's the kind of 'filling' Paul is referring to here: He uses the present passive imperative tense of the word *filled*, which means 'keep on being filled.' If you are allowing the Holy Spirit to control you, you are being filled by the Spirit." (Quoted from "Paul and the Prison Epistles" by Kathy Collard Miller and Larry Richards, Ph.D., page 98.)

Most Pentecostals would find themselves in agreement with much of this statement. For example, Pentecostals believe that at the moment of conversion, the new believer is immediately indwelt by the Holy Spirit, Who in this case is identified as the Spirit of Christ. Pentecostals would agree also that this "filling" is not a one-time event but is to be continual. The intent is clearly that we "keep on being filled." Furthermore, most Pentecostals would wholeheartedly agree that believers must surrender control to the Holy Spirit initially and continually.

However, Pentecostals would take issue with this "filling with the Spirit" being equated with living in obedience, as important as that is.

This passage is one of the core Scriptures which define Pentecostal theology, and in order to understand what Paul meant by this statement, one must first acknowledge that Paul held a Pentecostal or Charismatic theology. Biblical evidence is abundant that he was Spirit-filled, spoke in tongues and that his ministry was empowered by the Holy Spirit.

Pentecostal and Charismatic churches exist, at least in part, because of the differences in their beliefs about the role the Holy Spirit plays in the life of the believer and the life of the church.

First, let's address the issue of the role of the Holy Spirit in the conversion of a non-believer from an Evangelical/Pentecostal perspective. The Holy Spirit is the active agent in bringing the non-believer to an understanding of the gospel and salvation. Jesus said, "No man comes to Me unless the Father draws him," and we understand that to mean that it is the Father who draws, but the Holy Spirit, Who is the Spirit of God, is the Agent by which that drawing occurs.

The Holy Spirit, in the presence of the preaching of the gospel, convicts the unbeliever. That is, He convinces the sinner of the fact that he is guilty of breaking God's law, and, at the same time, reveals the righteousness of Christ and the judgment that is decreed against sin and sinners.

The recipient of the gospel message can then reject the

revelation or accept it. If he accepts the revelation, he will confess his sin, repent and receive by faith the forgiveness that God offers to all who believe on His Son. The new believer then experiences the witness of his spirit with the Holy Spirit that he is now a child of God.

In 1 Corinthians 3:16, Paul asks, "Do you not know that you are the temple of God and that the Spirit of God dwells in you?" In Romans 8:9, he states, "Now if anyone does not have the Spirit of Christ, he is not His." The terms "Spirit of Christ," "Spirit of God" and "Holy Spirit" seem to be used interchangeably in this context. There can be no doubt that the Scriptures proclaim that every believer is indwelt by the Holy Spirit from the moment of conversion.

However, Pentecostals and Charismatic believers differ from other Evangelicals in that they believe there is a second spiritual experience of being baptized in the Holy Spirit, which is distinct from and subsequent to conversion. Paul's testimony of his own spiritual experiences is a prime example.

No one seems to doubt that Paul was converted as a result of his encounter with Jesus on the road to Damascus and would have received the indwelling of the Holy Spirit at that time. However, three days later, Paul was visited by Ananias, whom the Lord had sent to him in order that his eyesight, lost in his Christ-encounter, would be restored and that he would be filled with the Holy Spirit. As a result of Ananias' prayer, Paul received his sight, and there is no reason to doubt he also received the fullness of the Spirit, fulfilling the entire prophetic vision. In 1 Corinthians 14, Paul confirmed that he spoke in tongues.

Another example of the baptism in the Holy Spirit occurring subsequent to salvation, and perhaps the clearest of all, is contained in the story of Philip's ministry in Samaria. In response to Philip's preaching and the accompanying miraculous signs, masses of Samaritan people were saved. Consequently, the Bible reads, "And there was great joy in that city." When the apostles and church leaders in Jerusalem heard of the Samaritan revival, they sent Peter and John to them to pray that they might receive the Holy Spirit, because they had been baptized in the name of Jesus but had not experienced the expected subsequent baptism in the Holy Spirit after their conversion experience.

Peter and John traveled immediately to Samaria, and when they laid hands on the Samaritan believers and prayed, they received the Holy Spirit.

This same sequencing of salvation, followed by Holy Spirit baptism, can be demonstrated in the original apostles (John 20:22 and Acts 2:1-4), the believers at Cornelius' house (Acts 10:44-48) and at Ephesus (Acts 19:1-10). Water baptism was also a part of the conversion, but sometimes it came before and sometimes after the baptism in the Holy Spirit.

Although Spirit baptism as an experience separate from salvation is important, and from a Pentecostal perspective, essential to the most effective Christian life, Spirit baptism is not a single experience. Initial Spirit

CHAPTER 17

baptism is, but it is also the beginning of a never-ending flow of the Spirit into and out of the believer.

We see this demonstrated several times in the Book of Acts. The first recorded example of a subsequent re-filling of the Spirit happened in response to the disciples' prayer for boldness to preach in the name of Jesus, despite the Jewish leaders having threatened them and forbidden them to do so. The Scripture records the following: "And when they had prayed, the place where they were assembled was shaken; and they were all filled with the Holy Spirit, and they spoke the word of God with boldness" (Acts 4:31).

A number of other Spirit fillings are recorded as the disciples faced trials and opposition to the gospel. In each case, they were filled afresh to enable them to meet and overcome the challenges. It was this ongoing availability of the Holy Spirit to meet the daily challenges of the Christian life and witness that Paul was admonishing the Ephesians to take advantage of when he wrote, "Be [continually being] filled with the Spirit."

The promise of the continuous infilling implicit in this command to be filled with the Spirit has not been withdrawn and is available to all believers in this day. There is a new dimension of effective service and witness for all who have experienced Spirit baptism and who continue to seek the infilling of the Spirit. It is the Holy Spirit that empowers the effective and victorious Christian walk in all its aspects. The Pentecostal baptism in the Holy Spirit has as its purpose the maximization of each believer's potential walk in the light and the wisdom of God.

Walk Under the Influence of the Holy Spirit

Here Paul is drawing a contrast between the alcohol-induced social environment of dissipation and sinful self-indulgence, and the believers' fellowship under the influence of the Holy Spirit. Those who would walk in wisdom will avoid alcoholic intoxication but will drink deeply of the Spirit. Those intoxicated with wine will exhibit gaiety, expressed in song and boisterous laughter, which does not edify but encourages further dissipation. When the effects wear off, nothing is left but physical pain and a sense of the futility of it all. Those that are filled or intoxicated with the Spirit of God will experience real joy, which can be productively expressed by the mutually edifying effects of singing spiritual songs and hymns which glorify God. These expressions will encourage those around us to join us in seeking Him, knowing Him and expressing our mutual thanks for all things.

"Speaking to one another in psalms and hymns and spiritual songs, singing and making melody in your hearts to the Lord" can be interpreted as a pattern for Pentecostal worship services. The psalms and hymns refer to the edification received when believers are gathered together and sing the Psalms and traditional hymns of the church.

"Spiritual songs" were probably spontaneous Spirit-inspired musical effusions, which have never been sung or heard before. This kind of spontaneous Spirit-inspired

CHAPTER 17

singing is a regular occurrence in some Pentecostal and Charismatic worship services. This is understood to be an example of Paul's declaration that "I will sing with the Spirit," which he differentiates from "singing with the understanding."

There seems to be an even wider application of this passage, in that we do not necessarily have to be in a corporate setting to speak to one another of spiritual things, and "making melody" in the heart would seem to be a productive activity which one can pursue at any time.

CHAPTER 18
SUBMISSION TO ONE ANOTHER

Ephesians 5:21:
Submitting yourselves to one another in the fear of God (KJV).

Submitting to One Another

"Submitting to one another in the fear of God" introduces the next great theme of Ephesians, which addresses submission in human relationships as a reflection of our submission to God.

The discussion of the various aspects of submission is a continuation of the exhortation for the Christian to walk worthy of his calling and being continually filled with the Spirit, which is necessary for success in these relationships.

One cannot understand the concept of biblical submission unless one first understands the concept of biblical authority. Submission and authority are inseparable and complementary, like two sides of the same coin. Both of these concepts, biblical submission and biblical authority, have come under heavy attack from society at large, and this resistance to biblical authority and submission has been exacerbated by erroneous teaching on these subjects within the church itself.

CHAPTER 18

<u>Human Authority Is Limited</u>

When considering the subject of submission and authority, one must first recognize that all authority rests ultimately in God Himself, Who is the Creator and Supreme Ruler of the universe. However, God has granted certain levels of authority to human individuals and institutions, but that authority is never absolute, and its limits are clearly defined. Romans 13:1-2 confirms this concept. "Let every soul be subject to the governing authorities. For there is no authority except from God, and the authorities that exist are appointed by God. [2]Therefore whoever resists the authority resists the ordinance of God, and those who resist will bring judgment on themselves."

The second thing we must recognize about God's delegated authority is that it is always granted for the purpose of *serving* those who are required to submit to the authority. God's authority is granted to enable the one holding the authority to serve others effectively. It is never granted for the benefit of the one to whom the authority is given. Authority must always be viewed as a tool by which service can be rendered.

Paul doesn't address it here, but God has constituted human government, referred to in the passage from the Letter to the Romans quoted above, for the purpose of serving those who are governed. One of the limiting parameters of human government is that it is not authorized to enact any law or issue any decree that would require conduct contrary to the revealed laws of God.

For example, human governments exceed their given authority when they require the worship of another god. Human governments are never given authority to require behavior that violates the moral law of God, such as the murder of one individual by another. The requirement in some countries that all pregnancies after the first live birth be terminated by abortion clearly exceeds the parameters of their God-given authority.

Neither can men as husbands and fathers, under the guise of biblical authority, require their wives or children to commit immoral or illegal acts. When the parameters of the God-given authority are exceeded, submission to these requirements can be rightfully and righteously resisted.

All authority except God's authority is limited; therefore, submission also has its limits.

Submitting Should be Mutual and Voluntary

Although Paul does not expand on the topic of submission to one another in any detail, a quick overview of the subject will enhance our discussion of the specific submission issues to follow.

There are a couple of ways to interpret this phrase, "Submit to one another," but before we go any further, it must be understood that submission in human relationships is supposed to be voluntary, based on trust and the anticipation of mutual benefit. No one is to be forced into submission. Biblical submission knows nothing of forceful subjugation. Voluntary submission means we willingly take our divinely ordained place in our relationships in the church, the marriage, the family and the workplace.

Submitting ourselves to one another could mean that we take our place in the hierarchy of the church structure of elders, bishops, pastors and deacons. However, this interpretation can lead to the imposition of a one-way, top-down flow of authority, removing the hierarchy from the mutual accountability God intended should be present in the church. This situation almost certainly will lead to the forceful subjugation of those under their authority. The early church with which Paul was familiar knew very little of this rigid structure. This would come centuries later as the church slipped away from its foundational principles and adopted a form of government similar to that of the Roman Empire. On the contrary, submission in the early church was recognized as intended to be mutual and voluntary.

Confirmation of this understanding is found in several New Testament passages. For example, Philippians 2:3-4 reads, "Let nothing be done through selfish ambition or conceit, but in lowliness of mind let each esteem others better than himself. [4]Let each of you look out not only for his own interests, but also for the interests of others." A second reference comes from 1 Peter 5:5: "Likewise you younger people, submit yourselves to your elders. Yes, all of you be submissive to one another." One last example from Romans 12:10 should be sufficient to prove the point: "Be kindly affectionate to one another with brotherly love, in honor giving preference to one another."

Mutual, voluntary submission to one another, regardless of role or position, was the expected norm in the church which Paul knew.

After passing over this broader issue of mutual submission without comment, Paul goes on to address three specific areas of submission. First, he addresses the love and submission required in marriage, using the love of Christ and the submission of the church as the model for this relationship. He then addresses the submission required of children to parents and finally the submission of slaves, or bondservants, to masters.

CHAPTER 19
SUBMISSION IN MARRIAGE

Ephesians 5:22-33:

Wives, submit yourselves unto your own husbands, as unto the Lord. [23]For the husband is the head of the wife, even as Christ is the head of the church: and he is the saviour of the body. [24]Therefore as the church is subject unto Christ, so let the wives be to their own husbands in every thing. [25]Husbands, love your wives, even as Christ also loved the church, and gave himself for it; [26]That he might sanctify and cleanse it with the washing of water by the word, [27]That he might present it to himself a glorious church, not having spot, or wrinkle, or any such thing; but that it should be holy and without blemish. [28]So ought men to love their wives as their own bodies. He that loveth his wife loveth himself. [29]For no man ever yet hated his own flesh; but nourisheth and cherisheth it, even as the Lord the church: [30]For we are members of his body, of his flesh, and of his bones. [31]For this cause shall a man leave his father and mother, and shall be joined unto his wife, and they two shall be one flesh. [32]This is a great mystery: but I speak concerning Christ and the church. [33]Nevertheless let every one of you in particular so love his wife even as himself; and the wife see that she reverence her husband (KJV).

Submission as an Expression of Love

The church is often referred to as the "bride of Christ" in the New Testament. In fact, Jesus Himself referred to His relationship with His disciples in terms of the Jewish wedding customs of His day, and Paul made his whole argument about the proper relationship of husbands and wives dependent on their understanding of the relationship between Jesus and the church. Wives are to submit to their husbands as their spiritual head, just as Christ, as its Head, is to receive the submission of the church.

Submission in Marriage is Voluntary

However, the submission required is not the forced submission to servitude, but the voluntary submission to acts of caring, protection and service. We submit to Christ because He loved the church so much that He sacrificed Himself for her that He might redeem her. Having bought her for Himself, He has also committed Himself to her preservation and welfare. This commitment was expressed in Jesus' words, "I will build My church and the gates of hell will not prevail against her" (Matthew 16:18).

Christ's work on behalf of the church is directed toward her perfection, or her sanctification. Christ gave Himself for the church, not just to redeem her from sin, but to make her holy, without imperfection, and fully conformed to His own image.

In saying that Jesus loved the church, Paul uses a form of "agape," which has already been defined as the love that

CHAPTER 19

is expressed in the promotion of the welfare of another, regardless of circumstances. "Agape" is not affected by the vicissitudes of feelings. Christ exercises His authority over the church for the benefit of the church, because He loves His church. Likewise, the husband exercises his authority over the wife for the benefit of the wife, because he loves her and is committed to the promotion of her welfare.

The husband is to love (promote the welfare of) his wife to no less extent that he loves (promotes the welfare of) himself. In fact, to fail to love the wife is a failure to love oneself. Paul says that failing to love one's wife is unnatural, for no one despises his own flesh, but nourishes it and cherishes it. Some psychiatrists believe that even when people abuse themselves and even kill themselves, they (perverted, though it may seem) believe they are somehow benefitting themselves.

Women are not to be subject to multiple heads. Women are subject only to Jesus and to their fathers, if unmarried, or to their husbands. They are not to be submitted to anyone else. Paul says it this way, "Wives submit to *your own husbands*, as unto the Lord."

A few years ago, the wisdom of this restriction was demonstrated in a dramatic way. In a large Charismatic church in a large metropolitan area, a horrible sex scandal was uncovered. Leaders, elders and pastors of this church were telling women that they should submit to their sexual advances because they were in spiritual authority over them, and the Bible required and blessed their submission. What a travesty! Just as the church is only required to submit to Christ, its Head and heavenly Bridegroom, the wife is only to be subject to Christ and her husband as he ministers to her and submits himself to Christ as his Head. The husband stands between the woman and all others who would try to exercise authority over her.

Paul uses two words in the closing of chapter 5 which are probably the most important words that can be applied in husband/wife relationships: love and respect. Recent marriage and psychological studies have proven that the most important thing in a man's life is to be respected, and the most important thing in a woman's life is to be loved.

Before we leave the subject of submission in marriage, please give your attention to the Appendix, a treatise on the concepts of love and respect in the marriage relationship.

Chapter 20
Children, Obey
Your Parents

Ephesians 6:1-4:

Children, obey your parents in the Lord: for this is right. ²Honour thy father and mother; (which is the first commandment with promise;) ³That it may be well with thee, and thou mayest live long on the earth. ⁴And, ye fathers, provoke not your children to wrath: but bring them up in the nurture and admonition of the Lord (KJV).

The Fifth Commandment

Paul couched this admonition in terms of the Fifth Commandment, "Honor your father and mother, that your days may be long upon the land which the Lord our God is giving you" (Exodus 20:12). However, he reinterprets it in broader terms for the Christian community by promising prosperity and long life to the individual child for obedience to this command. The original promise only referred to the Israelites as a people, and the implication was that they will only be able to stay in the land they were being given as long as they obeyed this command.

The inclusion of this promise in the original commandment points out how important obedience to this commandment is to God. God frequently told the

Israelites that failure to live by His Law would result in their being ejected from the land, but this is the only one of the Ten Commandments to which this threat of ejection is directly tied.

Obedience: In the Lord

Children are to obey their parents, however, the phrase "in the Lord" reminds us that parental authority is limited, and consequently, submission to parental demands for sinful behavior is not required. All God-delegated authority is given to enable the one in authority to love by promoting the welfare of those who are under his authority; therefore, any parent who coerces sinful behavior will be abusing his or her authority and will face the severest of God's judgments. Jesus said, "Whoever causes one of these little ones who believe in Me to sin, it would be better for him if a millstone were hung around his neck, and he were drowned in the depth of the sea" (Matthew 18:6-7).

Parental authority is granted to enable parents to love, serve and bring up their children in the nurture and admonition of the Lord. Submission to that authority is necessary so that service can be effectively rendered.

Reinforcement, Not Ridicule

The admonition to fathers to "not provoke your children to wrath" implies that parental actions can impede the children's ability and willingness to submit to authority. Perhaps a simple way to put this would be

CHAPTER 20

"Don't frustrate your children unnecessarily." In our relationship with our children, we must strive to eliminate destructive criticism, the imposition of unreasonable expectations and restrictions and the use of sarcasm and intimidation. Use of these tactics with children will provoke a child to wrath, resentment and downright disobedience. (Needless to say, use of these tactics in any relationship will not produce any long-term benefits to the serving authority.)

Instead, to remove barriers to obedience, we must emphasize recognition of accomplishments, encouragement, tenderness, patience, active listening, expressions of affection and continual affirmation of their value to you, the family and to God.

Teach the Word

Parents have the primary responsibility for the education of their children. They may delegate the task of teaching "Reading, 'Riting and 'Rithmatic" to professional teachers, but parents dare not rely on anyone other than themselves for the spiritual education of their children.

The words of Deuteronomy 6:6-7 are as important for today's Christian as they were for the Israelites of old. "And these words which I command you today shall be in your heart. You shall teach them diligently to your children, and shall talk of them when you sit in your house, when you walk by the way, when you lie down, and when you rise up."

Christian schools and church religious education

programs may assist parents in accomplishing this task, but the parents have the primary responsibility for passing on their faith to their children.

While the responsibility to teach the contents of the word of God is clearly declared, the strong implication from this passage is that parents, with fathers in the lead, must also teach by strong consistent example.

Joshua said, "As for me and my house, we will serve the Lord" (Joshua 24:14). Following his lead, fathers and husbands of today must take up their God-given responsibility to be the spiritual head of their families and, to the greatest possible extent, exert their influence on their wives and children to follow them as they follow the Lord.

The teaching of God's word in the family setting is essential, but living a life that is consistent with what is taught is equally, if not more, important.

Parents, Unite!

One of the greatest hindrances to a child's obedience is parents who are not in unity. First and foremost, parents must be in unity in following the Lord, and secondarily, they must be in unity regarding the discipline of their children. If the mother and father are divided about the direction the family should take and constantly undermine one another's authority, nothing but chaos is likely to result. A child cannot easily understand his place in God's divine order for the family if the parents are not taking their ordained place under God and in relationship to each other. If a child does not learn to take his place in the family, the basic foundational unit of all society, he will have even greater difficulty taking his proper place in society at large.

In the matter of discipline, once the parameters for the child's behavior are mutually agreed upon, the parents must also agree upon what consequences will be imposed on the child when those parameters are broken.

When some unprecedented infraction occurs, the parents should confer privately as to the action to be taken. Parents should never argue about disciplinary matters in front of the child, because the child will, almost certainly, try to manipulate this division for his own benefit and use this rift to escape punishment or get his own way.

Parents will also create a barrier to obedience if they do not always present a united front. Fathers, listen to your wife in these matters, and practice mutual submission. Nevertheless, God has given the husband — not the wife — the responsibility for assuring that the family follows a godly course.

<u>Be Consistent</u>

Whatever disciplinary course you take, be consistent. The two greatest rules in the discipline of children have to be "Don't abuse" and "Don't confuse."

First, let's consider how abuse creates a barrier to obedience. A good definition of discipline is "a controlled set of circumstances, designed to produce a mature and productive individual." Discipline is training, and sometimes training involves artificially imposing negative consequences to reinforce correct behavior. The imposition of these negative circumstances cannot be effectively imposed in anger. Discipline is not anger relief, but additional training. Negative circumstances decided upon and administered in anger can quickly escalate into abuse.

Any abuse will certainly provoke the child to wrath.

Now, let's consider "Don't confuse." Children will be confused by inconsistent rules and inconsistent actions by the parents in response to their breaking the rules. Unity and consistency are essential to avoid confusion. Parents, always do what you said you would do when you said you would do it. Idle threats encourage a child to disobey, and empty promises undermine the parent's credibility and make it difficult for the child to take anything the parent might say seriously.

Inconsistent application of discipline will provoke a child to wrath.

Remember, discipline is more about modifying future behavior than punishing past behavior. Effective discipline makes a clear distinction between disapproving bad choices and condemning the child's character. Assaulting a child's character by implying he is "bad" only communicates the parents' expectation of additional unacceptable behavior. Parents must learn that children can make bad choices out of immaturity and ignorance.

A prudent father and mother will prayerfully examine

their training methods and their imposition of
punishment to eliminate the possibility that their behavior
is somehow contributing to the lack of submission they
observe in their children.

Teach By Example

After saying, "Do not provoke your children to wrath,"
Paul says, "... *but* bring them up in the training and
admonition of the Lord." The connective "but" gives the
idea that the "training and admonition of the Lord" is the
opposite of provoking to wrath.

This certainly could imply that the "training and
admonition of the Lord" is more than the spoken word.
Perhaps this suggests that training and admonition alone
are not sufficient. Perhaps this should be taken as an
exhortation to add to the teaching a family environment
in which the training and admonition of the Lord is not
being violated. In other words, "Fathers, practice what you
preach."

The Greek word translated here, "provoke to wrath,"
can also be translated "to exasperate," "to anger" or "to
provoke." It can also be translated "to rouse to wrath,"
suggesting the idea of "to incite to rebellion."

Therefore, it appears that Paul is saying to the fathers,
"If you teach godly principles and then fail to adhere to
them yourself, you will incite your children to rebel
against you, your teaching and ultimately against God
Himself."

Sometimes the problem is not that children do not

obey their parents' teachings, but that they obey what is taught by example, rather than what is taught by the spoken word.

Children learn the importance of spiritual disciplines, prayer, Bible reading and church attendance from their observation of the importance their parents place upon these things.

Children learn to respect their elders when they observe their parents' elders being respected. Children learn to respect their pastors and church teachers when their parents also treat them with respect, even when differences of opinion may exist about issues facing the church.

Children learn to respect the law of the land when they observe their parents scrupulously obeying traffic laws, tax laws and hear them honoring and praying for those set in authority over them.

Consider this: Fathers, you are exerting influence all the time, by everything you do or fail to do, by everything you approve or fail to disapprove. The amount of time you spend declaring biblical truth to your children may be sufficient, but everything they know about you or see you do impacts their lives.

Creating and maintaining a godly environment is most important if you are to avoid inciting your children to rebellion.

Chapter 21
Submission in the Workplace

Ephesians 6:5-9:

Servants, be obedient to them that are your masters according to the flesh, with fear and trembling, in singleness of your heart, as unto Christ; [6]Not with eyeservice, as menpleasers; but as the servants of Christ, doing the will of God from the heart; [7]With good will doing service, as to the Lord, and not to men: [8]Knowing that whatsoever good thing any man doeth, the same shall he receive of the Lord, whether he be bond or free. [9]And, ye masters, do the same things unto them, forbearing threatening: knowing that your Master also is in heaven; neither is there respect of persons with him (KJV).

Submission Outside the Christian Context

Submission in an environment where there is at least some degree of commitment to loving one another is one thing, and even there, submission is sometimes difficult, but submission in an environment where this element is missing is quite another matter. Submission is hard enough when both parties are following Christ, but yet Paul says Christians must also submit in a work environment where frequently the goal is to extract as much from you as possible, at the least possible expense and without regard for your needs or desires. Paul has instructions for both Christian bondservants and slaves and Christian masters.

In Ephesus and throughout the Roman Empire, servitude and slavery were commonplace. However, with the advent of Christianity, something completely unprecedented was taking place. Both slaves and masters were accepting Christ as their Savior and Lord and were beginning to participate in worship together as equals in the church. Paul addressed this subject more fully in his letter to the Galatian church. "For you are all sons of God through faith in Christ Jesus. For as many of you as were baptized into Christ have put on Christ. There is neither Jew nor Greek, *there is neither slave nor free*, there is neither male nor female; *for you are all one in Christ Jesus*. And if you are Christ's, then you are Abraham's seed, and heirs according to the promise" (Galatians 3:26-29).

The Christian church turned Roman society on its ear. Equality to the extent practiced by the church was unprecedented. Becoming a Christian demanded changes in relationships. Christianity made submission to authority something that was to be freely given, not something extracted by force. Therefore, in the church, marriage and family relationships had to change, as well as the relationships between slaves and masters. These changes were mandatory for the believer, whether he was dealing with fellow believers or not.

Chapter 21

Adapting "Master-Slave" to "Employer-Employee"

Undoubtedly, the most difficult changes were those demanded of Christian slaves and Christian masters, who were now considered to be equal in Christ, and who were now expected to accept each other as friends, brothers and equals in the body of Christ. None of us today can relate directly to the master-slave scenario, but the principles of behavior Paul delineates for the master-slave relationship have a direct bearing on our modern employer-employee relationships.

Principles for the Christian Employee

The first principle is that submission and obedience is due to all masters, or employers, whether they are kind or not and whether they are Christian or not.

The principle that all God-ordained authority is limited applies to the master/employer the same as to all other arenas of authority. An employer has no more right than a husband, parent, church leader or government entity to demand a person violate a facet of the law of God.

A Christian slave, or employee, would be within his God-given rights to refuse such a demand without being condemned by God as a rebel. However, the ugly truth is that such refusals can and frequently do result in reprisals by the employing authority. For the slave in the Roman Empire, it could mean beatings or even death, for the master often had the power of life and death over his slaves.

For the Christian worker of today, dismissal or demotion could well be the result of refusing to comply with an order that violates his conscience. The words of Peter, while spoken in a different context, must be considered appropriate to this situation as well: "We must obey God rather than man." This must be the Christian's guiding principle whenever the demands of man and the will of God are in conflict.

On the other hand, the second and corollary principle is that to refuse to do the master/employer's lawful bidding is rebellion and brings a reproach on the worker and his Christian testimony.

The third principle is that employees are to give full effort on the job for which they are being paid. Submission in the workplace is not just saying, "Yes, Boss," but in being the best employee you can be. It means you give your full effort, all the time. It means you give 60 minutes of work for every hour you get paid. The Christian employee should meet or exceed every legitimate expectation the employer places on you. Submission by the Christian in the workplace leaves no room for slackness or laziness.

The term "not with eyeservice" means we are not to try to make ourselves look good, but to actually produce what is expected of you and more. Someone has said the Christian worker should be a source of profit for his employer, in that he actually produces more than he is being paid to produce. A Christian employee should work as diligently when he is not being observed as when the boss is looking over his shoulder. This is a matter of integrity and character. Character, as it has often been said, is what you are when no one is looking. Reputation is what other people think you are; character is what you know you are.

The fourth principle is that the Christian is to do everything as unto the Lord. Therefore, the Lord is ultimately the One to Whom you will answer for your conduct in the workplace, as well as in every other aspect of your life.

The Lord is every Christian employee's real "boss," and He is not only constantly observing every action, but He is also aware of every attitude of the heart.

Doing a good job at work is doing a good job for the Lord. The Christian is always in the Lord's service, regardless of the activity in which he may be involved at the time.

The fifth principle is that your faithful service to your employer will be rewarded by the Lord. We may not get the recognition or the raise, or we may miss a well-deserved promotion, but the Christian's reward for faithful service awaits us in heaven.

The reward for faithful service may, in fact, be more dependent on what we did at work that what we did at church. A Christian is a Christian all the time. He is never off duty in the Lord's service. He never has the option of abandoning the principles the Lord has given to guide his life.

Principles for the Christian Employer

As he nears the end of his discourse, Paul turns his attention to the masters, or employers: "… and you masters, do the same things to them." In other words, masters, employers, the same principles apply to you who are in authority as to those who are under authority.

While none of us own slaves or have indentured servants, many Christians do hold positions of authority in the workplace. Paul's admonition to the slave, or employee, was to do their work "as unto the Lord," and now to the employer he says, in effect, "Treat your employees as Christ would treat them."

Christ-like treatment of employees will include looking out for their legitimate needs. As a Christian boss, your employees are a sacred charge, and your dealings with them should bring no reproach to the name of Christ.

A Christian boss must be honest with his employees. It is a violation of integrity to pretend to be their advocate and then abandon them or sell them short to those in higher places of authority. God expects the employer to be faithful to the employee, just as God expects the employee to be faithful to his employer.

Lastly, Paul demands that Christian masters give up one of the most common methods of bringing a slave or bondservant into submission. He says, "Give up threatening." The word "threatening" could also be translated "menacing." The message is clearly that the instilling of fear under the threat of unjust physical or economic punishment is not acceptable as a means by which a Christian master exercises authority over those under his control. The message could be restated, "Stop beating your servants into submission, but rather be the kind of master to whom your servants will want to give their best efforts."

Jesus sets the example as the ideal Master. He will, of course, discipline His servants, but His primary method of motivation is not fear but love.

Christians love their Master because their Master first loved them and gave Himself for them. His approach is not with threats of damnation but with gifts of mercy and grace.

In our society, threats of physical punishment are not often found in the workplace; however, there are many ways an employer or boss can intimidate an employee: loss of the current position, loss of employment and bad performance reports which will impact future raises and promotions.

Finally, it must be noted that these kinds of employer and employee relationships, which allow for this mutual care and respect, can only be expected in Christian-to-Christian interactions, and further, in those Christian-to-Christian interactions where both parties are submitting to the will of God in the situation.

Even Christian employers may have to resort to threats of disciplinary actions with non-Christian employees. However, Christian employees, who are following Christ-like principles in their workplaces, should never find themselves in a place where they deserve the wrath of their employer.

The fact of the matter is that these relationships are complicated. Even among Christians there are no perfect employers or employees. The modern workplace is a foreign land where Christian principles may be viewed as weakness rather than strength. Regardless, the Christian must follow these principles and make amends when the inevitable failure comes. Christians are the light of the world, and they represent Christ, for good or ill, wherever they go. Therefore, it is incumbent on all believers, as much as depends on us by the help of the Holy Spirit, to adhere to our Christian principles, even in the workplace.

CHAPTER 22
BE STRONG IN THE LORD

Ephesians 6:10-12:

Finally, my brethren, be strong in the Lord, and in the power of his might. ¹¹Put on the whole armour of God, that ye may be able to stand against the wiles of the devil. ¹²For we wrestle not against flesh and blood, but against principalities, against powers, against the rulers of the darkness of this world, against spiritual wickedness in high places (KJV).

With this passage, Paul begins the third part of the simple "Sit, Walk, Stand" outline we imposed on the Letter to the Ephesians. This portion is a short but powerful explanation of our God-given ability to stand against the attacks of the evil one, using the metaphor of putting on the whole armor of God. The admonition to "be strong in the Lord" actually takes us back to the first part of the letter where Paul repeatedly refers to our spiritual position as being "in Christ." Again, here at the beginning of this passage on spiritual warfare and the protections we have been given, we find that our strength is "in the Lord." It is "in the Lord and in the power of His might" that we are able to maintain our position "in Him" and continue to "walk worthy of our calling," and ultimately "having done all to stand, stand."

Spiritual Warfare

The use of a Roman soldier's armor as an illustration and the reference to "withstanding all the fiery darts of the wicked one" alludes to what we call "spiritual warfare," a term that is never actually used in the Bible, but is all too evident in the life of all believers.

Over the past years, there has been an abundance of teaching on spiritual warfare. Nevertheless, debate continues to rage over just how much influence or power the devil has in the life of a Christian. There has been so much emphasis on this topic that many believers seem to spend more time focused on the devil and his influence than they do looking to Jesus, Who is the "Author and Finisher" of our faith.

It is Jesus who initiated our faith relationship with Him; it is He who sustains our faith relationship; and it is He Who will ultimately bring us to our final eternal reward and rest with Him. Paul's purpose here is not to extol the power and strategies of the devil, but to help us understand that "in Him," in Christ, we have all we need to be successful in defeating the most skillful attacks of our enemy.

Our Strength Is in Christ

We, in and of ourselves, may have no spiritual strength, but "in Him," by the power of His might, we can always be victorious. As Paul wrote to the Corinthians, "No temptation has overtaken you except such as is common to man; but God is faithful, who will not allow you to be tempted beyond what you are able, but with the temptation will also make the way of escape, that you may be able to bear it" (1 Corinthians 10:13). This is our promise, and no matter how severe the trial or how strong the attack, God will always provide a way by which we may come out of it victorious.

However, just because the way is provided, doesn't mean we will choose to take it. Sometimes God's "way to escape" requires a degree of obedience and self-denial that at the moment we are just not prepared to give. In this failure, the enemy succeeds in his attack, and we yield to the flesh, the result of which is sin. However, all is not lost. God in His mercy convicts us of our failure, and as John reminds us, "If we confess our sin, He is faithful and just to forgive us our sin and cleanse us from all unrighteousness" (I John 1:9).

Spiritual warfare is an ever-present reality. Every believer fights with the influence of society and its temptations to indulge the flesh at the expense of being obedient to the will of the Lord. We know that this battle is for the most part fought in the mind. The decision to obey God or yield to the sinful gratification of the flesh always comes down to decisions that we make in our minds.

Spiritual Battles Are Fought in the Spirit

Spiritual attacks often come through people who persecute us for our faith or actively resist our efforts to promote the kingdom of God. How we respond to these attacks comes down to a decision-making process, a battle, in the mind. The real test of our spiritual strength is not in the physical attack, but in how we respond to the attack.

When the spiritual attack is manifested in the physical realm, when people come against us, make life difficult for us, we have to understand that the real battle is on a different plane. It is on a spiritual plane, and the battle will not be won on any other plane. Spiritual attacks must be resisted in the Spirit, not in the flesh, or physical realm.

In fact, when we retaliate, seek vengeance or vindication in these physical manifestations of spiritual attacks, we play right into the enemy's hands. When we try to war in the flesh by seeking to win a physical or verbal battle with our physical attacker, we are attempting to take on the role of God.

The Scriptures tell us, "'Vengeance is mine,' says the Lord, 'I will repay'" (Deuteronomy 32:5). Humans, most particularly Christians, never fare very well when they try to do the things God has reserved unto Himself.

Even if we should best our physical opponent in a verbal or physical conflict, we, by winning the battle, actually lose the war. We battle not against flesh and blood, but against spiritual powers, and we can never win spiritual battles by physical efforts.

Some folks approach spiritual warfare as if Satan had not already been defeated and as if Satan's ultimate defeat is somehow dependent on their efforts. The Bible unequivocally declares that Satan is already defeated. Christ rose from the dead, signifying that He had won the

CHAPTER 22

victory over Satan and taken from him the keys of death, hell and the grave.

<u>Satan Is Defeated</u>

We are not required to defeat Satan — that has already been done — but we are required to resist him and stand firm in the face of his masquerade as a "roaring lion." But the key to avoiding falling victim to Satan's power to deceive, which is the only power left to him over the Christian, is not in direct resistance, but in the resistance that is the product of first having submitted ourselves to God. James' admonition to "Resist the devil and he will flee from you" cannot be understood properly without adhering to the admonition that immediately precedes it, "Submit yourselves therefore to God." It is only in the context of complete submission to God and His will that we will find the power to resist Satan and see him flee from us. Nothing has the power to repel the devil like one who is completely submitted to God.

Spiritual warfare is not our primary responsibility or purpose. Our sole responsibility is to "seek first the kingdom of God and His righteousness." In the process of seeking the kingdom, we will encounter Satan in any number of guises as he seeks to keep us distracted from our primary goal. We are not even primarily responsible for the building of the kingdom of God, because Jesus said, "I will build My church, and the gates of hell will not prevail against it." As we yield ourselves to the Lord and seek to do His will, He will use us in the building of His church. We are not the architects or even the builders; we are more like the tools in His hands that He uses to accomplish His purposes.

We Are Victorious

We are "in Christ," and naturally we are going to feel the heat of the battle since we are the body of Christ, but the success of the enterprise is assured. Satan is defeated, and although God has, for his own reasons, given Satan permission to continue to rule on the earth for a time, God uses him as an instrument for the testing and proving of our faith. Our ability to live in victory over all the schemes, wiles and attacks of Satan is in Christ. Our victorious resistance by the grace and power of God is a greater source of glory to God than if Satan were to be removed from the scene. In a funny sort of way, even Satan's attacks are a means to the glorification of our God.

We know that the corporate body of Christ, the church, will not and cannot be defeated in accomplishing its primary task, and it is guaranteed by the words of Jesus to obtain the ultimate victory. However, the individual member of the body of Christ still faces his or her own private battle against the evil one. In this passage, Paul has given believers two means by which we can maintain the flow of the power and might of our Lord through our lives, confound the enemy's schemes and quench every fiery dart thrown against us: putting on the armor of God and prayer.

CHAPTER 22

"Fiery Darts" and Discipline

It is important that we understand the difference between the "fiery darts" of the enemy and the discipline of the Lord. Many believe that all of life's negative circumstances are from the devil and his minions. They consider all sickness, accidents, financial reverses and broken relationships to be the result of satanic or demonic attack. However, there are two facts that we must always keep in mind: All negative circumstances are not from the devil, and all positive circumstances are not from the Lord.

Negative circumstances can be from the Lord in order to correct current disobedient behavior. A good example is found in the story of Jonah. Negative circumstances can also come from the Lord as a means of discipline, keeping in mind that discipline is not to be considered primarily as punishment, but rather as training. However, discipline may have elements of chastisement, as the 12th chapter of the Epistle to the Hebrews relates.

The Greek word used for chastisement is "paideia," but its primary meaning is: tutorage; nurture; education or training. Only secondarily and by implication does it have the connotation of disciplinary correction. God is primarily concerned with our spiritual maturation, not assuring us a pain- and trouble-free life. He is more concerned with our spiritual fruitfulness than our comfort.

Jesus, in one of His final discourses before going to the cross, related the parable in which He said, "I am the vine, you are the branches" (John 15:5). In this parable, He stresses the fact that God, the Husbandman, prunes the branches so that they begin to bear fruit, then to bear more fruit and finally, to bear much fruit.

Pruning is the process of cutting away the things that take away from the ability to bear fruit. For the Christian, bearing fruit is defined as developing the character of Christ and doing the will of God. This process, when experienced in human flesh, cannot be assumed to be painless.

On the other hand, every positive circumstance we encounter does not necessarily come from the Lord. Satan, who has the ability to appear as an angel of light, can also create the illusion of all sorts of positive circumstances to deceive and ensnare us. To take advantage of every promotion or every opportunity to improve our lifestyles does not necessarily come from God, but may be from the enemy to divert our attention from what God actually wants for us.

Not every financial windfall will prove to be a blessing, unless it is used properly. It could very well be a test of our stewardship. The rich man of Jesus' parable thought that his abundant harvest was a blessing he was to hoard away, but God dealt severely with him because he fell for the temptation to trust in the provision rather than the God who made the provision.

In life, we see things as positive or negative based on our limited human perspective. What seems good today may prove to be bad as time goes by. On the other hand, what initially seems to be a serious negative circumstance may prove to be a blessing in disguise.

Fiery darts may not always be fiery in appearance. Many a fiery dart has come in disguise. The devil is the master of the Trojan horse maneuver.

CHAPTER 23
THE WHOLE ARMOR OF GOD

Lee pg. 163

Ephesians 6:13-17:

Wherefore take unto you the whole armour of God, that ye may be able to withstand in the evil day, and having done all, to stand. [14]Stand therefore, having your loins girt about with truth, and having on the breastplate of righteousness; [15]And your feet shod with the preparation of the gospel of peace; [16]Above all, taking the shield of faith, wherewith ye shall be able to quench all the fiery darts of the wicked. [17]And take the helmet of salvation, and the sword of the Spirit, which is the word of God: (KJV).

Putting on the Whole Armor of God

In the recent past, there has been a lot of emphasis on a ritualistic application of this concept. Some teach that a believer should recite this Scripture every day and say to himself, "I put on the helmet of salvation, etc., etc."

This is probably not what Paul had in mind, because every piece of armor he describes relates metaphorically to a facet of Christ's ministry to His followers. Taken all together, the pieces of the armor give us a portrait of Christ and a description of His ongoing work on our behalf.

172

CHAPTER 23

In fact, this description of the armor of God and its relationship to the work of Christ really takes us back to the earlier part of this letter where Paul repeatedly talks about the saints being "in Christ." In effect, we have come full circle. We have been placed in Christ, and this description of the armor of God is just another way of saying that "in Christ" we have protection from the enemy of our souls.

With all metaphors, it is possible to extend them too far and thus confuse the simple message it was originally meant to convey. Any attempt to read spiritual significance into the relationship between a particular part of the armor and the part of the body it protects may be such an over-extension. Therefore, unless it is obvious there is a connection between the specific piece of armor and the particular area of the body it covers, no speculative connection should be attempted.

As we look at each piece of the armor of God, our primary focus will be to see in it a representation of the work of Christ on our behalf.

The Girdle of Truth

The "girdle of truth" reminds us of Jesus' description of Himself as "the way, the truth and the life." Jesus is not only witness to the truth, He is the embodiment of the ultimate truth of who God is, what He is like and how He has planned and provided for the redemption of sinful man.

The Breastplate of Righteousness

The Roman soldier's breastplate was constructed of leather and metal and protected his vital organs. It was intended to prevent the soldier from sustaining a mortal wound. In the same manner, believers, clad in the righteousness of Christ, will suffer no mortal wound in their battles with their enemy.

The "breastplate of righteousness" reminds us that Jesus is our righteousness. We have no righteousness of our own; however, when we are born again, we are clothed in the righteousness of Christ by faith.

When speaking of the righteousness of Christ, we also use the metaphor of being covered with the blood of Jesus. This reminds us of the practice of the High Priest, who once a year took the blood of the sacrifice into the Holy of Holies and sprinkled the blood on the Atonement Cover, or Mercy Seat, of the Ark of the Covenant. God declared that He would be present in the area above the Mercy Seat and between the wings of the cherubim. The blood sprinkled by the High Priest was interposed between the holiness of God and the stone copy of the Law contained in the chest below. The blood "covered" the sins of the Israelites, representing how the blood of Jesus now covers our sin. So we get the idea that as God looked down, all He saw was the atoning blood, not the broken covenant. Just so, as God looks down on us, He sees the blood of Jesus, not our sin.

Blood of Christ

174

CHAPTER 23

<u>Feet Shod With the Gospel</u>

"Having shod your feet with the preparation of the gospel of peace" does not refer to a preparation that must be accomplished, but a preparation that is already complete and available for use. For example, at the direction of a physician, a pharmacist will prepare a medication or an ointment for our use. This "preparation" requires no additional work on our part, other than to apply it in the prescribed way. The gospel is complete and requires no additions or modifications, but is ready to be applied.

It has been frequently said that the only offensive weapon in the "armor of God" is the "sword of the Spirit." However, the shoes of the Roman soldier were heavy enough to sustain them in marching over the roughest terrain and may have also contained metal studs to enhance traction. These shoes could be used in a number of offensive applications, including kicking an opponent into submission. There is a certain amount of satisfaction in knowing that when the devil is under our feet, he is crushed by the "gospel of peace."

When we think of the "preparation of the gospel of peace" in association with the feet, we are reminded that we have been given the "gospel of peace" and are commanded to "go into the world and preach the gospel to every creature."

The gospel has been supplied to us, and with this gospel we are able to stand, regardless of the circumstances in which we may find ourselves. When the

Lord gives the order to move out against the enemy, we can do so in confidence.

The Shield of Faith

Paul then says we are to "above all, take the shield of faith." The use of the term "above all" is usually understood as referring to the priority of faith in all spiritual matters, and, of course, we cannot be "in Christ" nor have His strength or protection available to us without first having believed in Him. So, it is true that everything begins with faith in God. However, in this metaphor, the shield of faith refers to the function of the Roman foot soldier's shield, which was constructed of alternate layers of metal and leather. It was about four feet tall and wide enough to cover his whole body. Since the average Roman soldier was around five feet tall, he could easily crouch behind his shield and be completely protected from all sorts of projectiles, including the "fiery darts of the enemy."

The Greek word "en," which most Bibles translate as "above," is a preposition with a wide range of possible interpretations. In this case, one might come closer to Paul's intended message if the phrase were translated "over all," in the sense of "covering everything." Faith — the absolute trust in God, His goodness and His ability to work all things together for the believer's development — is the first line of defense against every attack.

Chapter 23

The Helmet of Salvation

The last piece of defensive armor listed is the "helmet of salvation." There is only one other reference to the helmet of salvation in the Bible. Paul may have had the following passage from Isaiah 59:17 in mind when he wrote this: "For He put on righteousness as a breastplate, and a helmet of salvation on His head."

Although Isaiah was referring to the Lord putting on these items, the application to the believer is appropriate, for the helmet protects the head, which is the seat of our thought life. Every spiritual battle is fought, first of all, in our minds. When temptations, trials and testings come, we make the choice in our minds to follow the desires of our own will or to follow the will of God. We always _decide_ what we are going to do before we _do_ what we decided.

Satan's attacks target our minds and emotions, and we know that with every temptation God has already provided a means of escaping the temptation. As a result of being saved, we have a new nature. This new nature, enabled by the Holy Spirit, can take authority over the old nature, which is subject to enticement by Satan and his evil forces. Satan uses the circumstances of our lives and the false hope of an improved situation to tempt the believer to follow his own will instead of the will of God.

That's how Eve got hooked. She was living in the Garden of Eden, the best of all possible earthly situations, yet the devil was able to deceive her into believing that she could improve her circumstances by disobeying God.

Satan misrepresented God to her as one who did not have her best interests in mind and that He was withholding something from her that would greatly enhance her life. Satan attacked her mind, deceived her and altered her perception of God.

In Christ, our minds are protected by the helmet of our salvation. While we may still choose to believe the lie and act on it, we can be sure that the Holy Spirit faithfully pointed us to the truth. We stand with the power of decision between the Holy Spirit, Who urges and empowers us to choose to obey God, and Satan, who offers us the false hope of betterment by following our own desires. Satan's argument is always that we actually can make better decisions on our own than by following God's will. The helmet of salvation is the means by which we discern and follow the truth of God.

The Sword of the Spirit

In this inventory of the believer's armor, the last item is the "sword of the Spirit," which is the word of God. The word of God, which we take primarily to mean the Bible, actually may have a broader meaning, for certainly, the New Testament, as we know it, was not yet complete when the Letter to the Ephesians was written. For Paul, the word of God would have included the Old Testament, the gospel as preached by Jesus to the disciples and through his own special revelation from Jesus. While the word of God for us is primarily the Bible as we now have it, God is continually speaking to the followers of Jesus and making specific application of that written word to their personal walk with the Lord. At other times, God may, in consonance with His written word, give the believer personal, specific directions or a promise that only applies to him or her. Knowing what God has called us to do and knowing the promises He has made to us personally are powerful weapons in turning back the attacks of the enemy.

Jesus serves as our example of using the word of God to deflect the attacks of the enemy. On each occasion when He was tempted by Satan in the wilderness, Jesus refuted the appeals of Satan by quoting from the Scriptures. In this application, the word of God was used in a defensive manner; however, when we preach the gospel, we are using it as an offensive weapon. For it is by the preaching of the word of God that the influence of Satan is broken in the lives of unbelievers. It is by hearing the word of God that they are set free from the kingdom of darkness and brought into the kingdom of light.

Chapter 24
Praying in the Spirit

Ephesians 6:18:

Praying always with all prayer and supplication in the Spirit, and watching thereunto with all perseverance and supplication for all saints; (KJV).

Paul follows his discussion of standing in the whole armor of God with an appeal for the Ephesians to be "praying always, with all prayer and supplication in the Spirit." While we primarily think of "always" as meaning "all the time or continually," it can also be interpreted as "by all ways, means or methods."

When taken in the sense of praying continually, we understand it to mean that prayer should be a regular and consistent activity. Prayer must never fail to be a routine practice. When taken in the sense of praying "in all ways," it is understood to incorporate private devotional prayer and public or corporate prayer. It can mean praying silently or aloud. "In all ways" certainly must be understood to refer to the ability every Spirit-filled believer has to "pray in the Spirit" as opposed to "praying with the understanding."

"Praying with the understanding" is prayer coming as a result of calling to mind needs which we have previously been made aware. "Praying in the Spirit" is using the

CHAPTER 24

ability to speak in tongues, which came as the initial physical evidence of Spirit baptism. We "pray in the Spirit" when the Spirit of God moves upon our spirit to pray without our minds being involved in the process. Paul said in his Letter to the Corinthians, "What is the conclusion then? I will pray with the spirit, and I will also pray with the understanding. I will sing with the spirit, and I will also sing with the understanding" (1 Corinthians 14:15). Although the translators of the New King James Version did not capitalize the references to the Spirit, from the context it is evident that it is the Holy Spirit Paul has in mind.

In 1 Corinthians 14, Paul makes it clear that one who speaks in tongues speaks to God. Speaking to God, for the Christian, almost always means praying to Him or giving praise to Him. Paul confirms the fact that speaking in tongues is prayer or praise when he says that anytime tongues is spoken in the congregation, an interpretation must be given, otherwise the others present will not be able to say "Amen" to the giving of thanks.

Praying in the Spirit is most likely in view in Romans 8:26: "Likewise the Spirit also helps us in our weakness. For we do not know (in our understanding) what we should pray as we ought, but the Spirit Himself makes intercession for us with groanings which cannot be uttered." This can be applied in two ways.

First, we may be aware of a need, but have no idea what the resolution of the need should be, therefore, we do not know how to pray. By using the prayer language, or praying in the Spirit, the Holy Spirit uses the believer to pray to the Father with the understanding of the Spirit of God. Since the Spirit of God cannot construct a prayer in opposition to the will of God, the prayer in the Spirit will always be in the divine agreement that guarantees the answer.

On the other hand, in the second instance, the Spirit may lead us to intercede for needs of which we have no natural way to be aware. There are hundreds of testimonies of people who suddenly felt an almost irresistible urge to pray for a specific person, although they had no idea of the person's current situation. Not knowing how to pray, they prayed in tongues, using their "prayer language." Later, some of them have found that the person for whom they felt the urge to pray was in some imminent peril from which they were miraculously delivered.

On two separate occasions, my wife has been awakened with a strong urge to pray for a particular soldier who was deployed, first to Iraq and then to Afghanistan. In both incidents, his life was in peril. The first time, as he was defusing an IED, the devise exploded. To the astonishment of those present, he was immediately seen walking out of the smoke and debris of the explosion without a single injury. The second incident involved his escaping unharmed from an attack which left five other members of his unit dead.

Paul calls for prayer and supplication. Supplication is essentially the same as prayer, but perhaps with the connotation of increased intensity.

CHAPTER 25
UNITY IN THE ESSENTIALS

Ephesians 6:19-20:

And for me, that utterance may be given unto me, that I may open my mouth boldly, to make known the mystery of the gospel, ²⁰For which I am an ambassador in bonds: that therein I may speak boldly, as I ought to speak (KJV).

As Paul comes to the end of his admonitions for the Ephesians to pray, he calls for them to persevere in prayer for themselves, for all the saints and for him. In this, Paul emphasized that prayer is not to be focused on oneself only, but for fellow believers and ministers of the gospel.

Paul's appeal for prayer for himself is "that I might open my mouth boldly to make known the mystery of the gospel for which I am an ambassador in chains." This "mystery of the gospel" has been one of his main themes in this letter, and it remains the central focus of the ministry to which Jesus had called him and made him "an ambassador," or a "representative of the ruling authority."

The mystery of the gospel as Paul understood it was that God was bringing about His eternal plan to reconcile people of all kindred tribes and tongues into one body. He understood God had created one spiritual family in His Son, Jesus, Who had been sent to be the final and complete sacrifice for the sin of all people, worldwide.

For Paul, there was only one body, one Spirit, one hope, one Lord (Jesus Christ), one faith, one baptism, one God and Father of all. Because of this commonality of belief, there was no room for any division in the church. Unlike Paul, today, we are not so concerned about the issue of whether Jews and Gentiles are one in the body of Christ. Most Christians agree, in principle at least, that all who are truly in Christ by faith are part of one body of Christ.

Our struggle with unity in the body of Christ presents itself in a different guise. Today, there are many thousands of independent groups, denominations and cults, all of which claim to be Christian, yet their faith statements and doctrinal creeds are at times radically different from each other and from the time-honored interpretations of the Bible itself. And while the so-called body of Christ continues to divide itself, there is also a call for putting aside our doctrinal differences and uniting in our efforts to promote the growth of Christianity. After all, Jesus prayed in the Garden of Gethsemane that His followers would be one, just as He and the Father are one.

The great question that must be resolved before Christians can find a true unity is "What are the essences of Christianity?" In other words, "What are the essential doctrines of the faith?" Having come to an understanding of this issue, we must continue to be ambassadors of that faith.

One of the concepts that has arisen in the debate between Evolutionism and Creationism is the concept of

CHAPTER 25

"Irreducible Complexity." Irreducible Complexity is the concept that, in any system, biological or mechanical, certain elements must be present at the same time and in their proper relationships for the system to work. A simple example is the airplane. The essential elements of an airplane are wings, fuselage, tail assembly, engine and propeller. If one of these elements is missing or not properly placed, the airplane will not fly. Obviously, airplanes have many more components than these, but they are not essential to its ability to fly.

In our efforts to come into some sort of ecumenical unity, we must determine what are the essential elements of Christianity, what are the essential beliefs and actions that enable Christianity to "fly."

Paul begins the Epistle to the Ephesians by stressing their position "in Christ." Once a person is "in Christ," the outflow from his life will change and reflect the nature of the one of whom he has become a part. Consequently, it is of the greatest importance to know how one gains the position of being "in Christ," and beyond that, "How does one maintain that status?"

Some denominations believe they secure their position "in Christ" by infant baptism. Some believe that salvation is only possible through membership in a particular religious organization. Still others believe that their position in Christ is the result of their having been born again by faith in Jesus Christ. However, Christianity really doesn't fly on that basis alone. As James tells us so forcibly, "Faith without works is dead." Christianity cannot be defined in terms of a single experience. The initial conversion experience must be followed by a life of dedicated discipleship to Christ.

One certainly enters into Christ by being born again by faith, but if being born again, having a new nature, being converted, is to have any practical meaning, a new lifestyle must emerge as a result. Believers in Jesus must be followers of Jesus. The second major segment of the Epistle to the Ephesians is Paul's attempt to define what that new lifestyle, or that walk, will begin to look like as one matures in his relationship with the Savior.

As he concludes the description of the new lifestyle that flows out of the new position the believer has in Christ, Paul assures the Ephesians that not only does their position in Christ produce a new life, it also provides them with all the protection they need to maintain their position and lifestyle. However, their position, although secure in the person of Christ as pictured by the whole armor of God, is not totally unassailable. Consequently, he warns them to be persistent in prayer and to always be vigilant and watchful. Although Satan and sin have no real power over them, they are still subject to the incredible deceptive power of the evil one. In this, Paul echoes the warning of Peter in his first letter, "Be sober, be vigilant; because your adversary the devil walks about like a roaring lion, seeking whom he may devour. Resist him, steadfast in the faith, knowing that the same sufferings are experienced by your brotherhood in the world" (1 Peter 5:8-10).

CHAPTER 25

As Christians we must know the essence of the gospel. We must know how to come "into Christ." We must also understand what the essential biblical elements are of the walk that the Spirit will lead us on.

This essential knowledge will come only as we pray, study God's word and listen to the Spirit's leading. Then we have a responsibility to boldly make known the mystery of the gospel and be bold ambassadors of the truth. We may join with others in this effort, but only with those who hold to the essential elements of Christian doctrine and show evidence of a practical application of those doctrines.

We all have a responsibility to contend for the faith. As Jude 3 tells us, "Beloved, while I was very diligent to write you concerning our common salvation, I found it necessary to write to you exhorting you to contend earnestly for the faith which was once for all delivered to the saints."

In order to walk in unity with Christians affiliated with other organizations, we must be sure we agree on the essential elements of the faith, but before we exclude anyone from our fellowship, we must also be sure we are not guilty of engaging in "doubtful disputations" about matters of preference, rather than essential core values of the gospel.

As St. Augustine said, "In the essentials, unity; in doubtful things, liberty; but in all things, love."

CHAPTER 26
A FINAL GREETING

Ephesians 6:21-24:

But that ye also may know my affairs, and how I do, Tychicus, a beloved brother and faithful minister in the Lord, shall make known to you all things: [22] Whom I have sent unto you for the same purpose, that ye might know our affairs, and that he might comfort your hearts. [23] Peace be to the brethren, and love with faith, from God the Father and the Lord Jesus Christ. [24] Grace be with all them that love our Lord Jesus Christ in sincerity. Amen (KJV).

As Paul ends his Letter to the Ephesians, his greatest concern was that the Ephesians would not be discouraged or disheartened by his imprisonment. Apparently, he intends for Tychicus, "a beloved brother and faithful minister in the Lord," to carry his letter to them by hand. Paul was concerned that his letter, as encouraging as it was, might not be enough to allay their fears regarding his imprisonment.

Tychicus, by his presence, would be able to assure them that Paul, although in chains, was not in dire distress.

In fact, Paul saw his imprisonment as a unique opportunity to preach the gospel in a venue that would have ordinarily been closed to him.

CHAPTER 26

Paul wanted the Ephesians to know everything about his current situation and to be encouraged. Paul lived his life as an open book. He was fully accountable to his brothers and sisters in the Lord. In this way, he set a great example for all Christians and particularly for ministers of the gospel.

In closing, he pronounced blessings upon them. He spoke of peace and love with faith, which he believed God would grant them. He called for God's grace, God's active work for their good, to be theirs.

Finally, Paul's last thought called to their attention the essentiality of loving the Lord Jesus Christ with sincerity. For those who are in Christ, loving Him with their whole heart, mind and soul is the only acceptable measure of devotion and the only means to experience the fullest extent of God's peace, love and grace.

Appendix

Love and Respect
By Rebecca Shaw, PhD.

Ephesians 5:33 suggests that God knew from the beginning not only that women would have difficulty understanding the essence of *respect* for their husbands, let alone showing respect to them, but also that men would have difficulty understanding and *loving* their wives as Christ loves the church.

Love and Respect: The God-created Man/Woman Relationship

Genesis 2 tells us that in the beginning, God placed *the man*, Adam, in the Garden of Eden to tend and keep it. He *commanded the man* not to eat of the tree of the knowledge of good and evil, for if he did eat of this tree "you," the man, would "surely die." The Lord God then said it was not good for the man to be alone so he created a "helper comparable to him." He then caused Adam to fall into a deep sleep and took a rib from him. God made the rib into a woman and "brought her to the man." They, the man and the woman, became one, enjoying the perfect garden. God had created women for men.

Love and Respect: The Change in Relationship Roles

It appears in Genesis 3 that Adam had told his wife about God's command, not to eat of the tree of knowledge. However, based on the woman's response to the serpent who tempted her to eat the fruit, it is unclear whether Adam added to God's command when he explained it to the woman or the woman expanded the command of her own volition. Either way, her interpretation and understanding of the command and ultimate consequences were erroneous, making her vulnerable to being easily manipulated and deceived by the most "cunning beast of the field which the Lord God had made." The serpent used flattery, smooth talk, to the woman, "… your eyes will be opened … you will be like God … you will know good and evil." She looked at the tree and saw it was good for food, it was pleasant to the eyes and able to make one wise. She ate the fruit and gave it to her husband of which he ate. Immediately, their eyes were opened, and when they heard God walking in the garden in the cool of the day, they hid themselves among the trees of the garden; they hid from His presence because they knew what they had done was wrong in the eyes of God.

God called Adam out, asking him if he had eaten of the tree of which He commanded him not to eat. Immediately, Adam threw his wife under the bus. "The woman whom You gave to be with me, she gave me of the tree and I ate." God confronted the woman, and she blamed the serpent. "The serpent deceived me, and I ate."

At that moment, the world order was changed forever. The roles between husband and wife and the family rules changed immediately. God said to the woman, "Your desire shall be for your husband, and he shall rule over you." To the man, God said the ground would be cursed for his sake. It would produce thorns and thistles; he would *toil* all the days of his life. His life would be contentious, challenging. Adam would rule over Eve. Man would rule over woman, husband over wife. The essence of love and respect changed that day. Man and woman have struggled with lack of contentment ever since.

Love and Respect: The Deterioration of the God-created Relationship

For centuries women have been trying to obtain "Love" from their men, and men have been trying to obtain and at times demand "Respect" from their women. There are many examples in the Bible demonstrating the deterioration of love and respect within marital relationships.

In the Book of Esther, King Ahasuerus had a lavish feast with lots of important guests. He wished to show off his lovely wife, Queen Vashti, who made her own feast in the royal palace for the women. The king *commanded* his wife to join him in order to "show her beauty to the people and the officials for she was beautiful to behold." The queen refused, and the king became furious. With the help of those around him, the king developed a decree proclaiming throughout his empire that "all wives will honor their husbands, both great and small." He wanted to be sure that "each man should be the master in his own house." In addition, King Ahasuerus made another royal decree which first prohibited his wife from coming before him and second gave her royal position to another "who is better than she." The queen was eventually disposed of and replaced by Esther.

In the book of Judges, Samson's wife manipulated him to tell her the secret to a riddle he had proposed to a group of men in exchange for some clothing and linen garments. In a threatening manner, the men enticed Samson's wife to get the answer to the riddle. She *wept* on Samson for days, stating, "You only hate me! You do not love me!" After days of listening to her, Samson told her the answer, which she promptly gave to the men of the city. Samson became very angry, and his "wife was given to his companion, who had been his best man."

There are plenty of examples in the Bible which clearly demonstrate the degeneration of love and respect within marital relationships. The deterioration has taken place largely because of power and control, partners vying for the ultimate control.

Love and Respect: The Critical Component of Love and Respect is Having a God-centered Heart

The reality is neither love nor respect can be "obtained" or "demanded" because both come from the heart, an attitude of the heart. Love and respect are birthed from a God-centered heart. This is why a godly husband can use kind words to a wife with a sword-like tongue; why a godly wife can continue to build a husband up when he constantly tears her down. Many of us, when we see these types of scenarios play out in front of our eyes, shake our heads and wonder, "Why does she/he put up with that?" We predict, "If he ever does that to me, I'll slap him silly or I'll kick him to the curb. I deserve better than that." And it may be true that you've been a good servant to others; however, more often than not, servant-hood has come out of self-righteousness, not humbleness. Our sanctimonious self-talk is something like, "I cleaned the toilet again, the least he could do is take care of the kids for a while" or "I bought her a vacuum cleaner last week, the least she could do is stop nagging about the broken faucet."

Love and Respect: Ways Men Fail to Love and Women Fail to Respect

Self-righteousness. Our self-righteous attitude allows us to forget, rationalize and justify the ugliness we, too, have shown toward others. Most importantly, we don't acknowledge the ugliness, the disrespect and unlovingness we've shown toward God, despite His love for us as shown through His selfless sacrifice on the cross. When we allow ourselves to deny, rationalize, minimize and justify our own weaknesses, we become more and more self-righteous. We demand specific responses, actions and attitudes from others, and we give to others only when certain conditions are fulfilled.

What we seem to forget is that love and respect are not about one's self. Rather they are about having a godly heart. As Matthew 20:28 states, "For the Son of Man did not come to be served, but to serve." No matter what others did to hurt Him, He came to the world to serve. Through His service, He displayed love and respect to all, both His friend and foe. Despite having been rejected, spit upon and beaten by many, He chose to give His life, while we were yet sinners, so that *some* could spend eternity with Him.

Lack of effort. Most people begin marriages with good intentions, putting significant effort into placing the needs of their partner first, using positive words to build up their partner and eliciting input from their partner before making a decision. However, after a while, this amount of effort becomes tiresome amidst the daily needs of life. The energy to meet the daily demands supersedes the good intentions. For many, emotional baggage from childhood and adolescence eventually begins to interfere with the good intentions as emotional and physical energy becomes more and more depleted and attention is diverted to meet demands of everyday life. When this happens, priorities change, and often attitudes of love and respect become less and less important. Attitudes of power and control, wanting it your way, become more and more important.

Power struggles. Countless couples find themselves in needless power struggles. They vie for power often because they perceive themselves as losing control in one or more areas of their lives. As each partner fights for power and control, a battle ensues, and frequently an intricate *winner* and *loser* dance develops … the battle dance.

Love and Respect: Downward Spiral of the Battle Dance

The *battle dance* becomes more seductive and elaborate as each person meticulously hones their swords for battle and fine-tunes their strategic plans of attack. The tongues of fire burn hotter and deeper, and the tactics become more deceptive. When one partner withdraws, the other partner will attack. The battle dance becomes more and more intense as the fires burn out of control, each partner believing they are advancing toward their goal, gaining power and control.

What most couples do not understand is that power and control do not come through battle. Rather, they come through surrendering, letting go of power and control. Often, power and control are about being *right*, and being right often translates into "I'm going to show you that I'm right, no matter the cost."

The battle dance is prolonged because people don't realize or don't take responsibility for their own power and control issues. Instead they point the finger at their partner. "If only he would …" or "If only she would …" The speck in the partner's eye becomes the focus, rather than the plank in one's own eye. The *blame* attack is only one of many strategic steps in the battle dance.

Another dance step in the battle occurs when one or both partners *focus on negative aspects* of the partner and/or the relationship, *discounting positive characteristics*. This move slows down the flow of the dance, frustrating the partners. Often, the positive partner becomes overwhelmed with a pessimistic attitude and lashes out with either anger or tries to protect by withdrawing. This process results in bitterness which poisons within, causing a greater gap between the marital partners.

Catastrophizing is another dance step, and it begins when one partner, or both, makes small challenges into big problems. It can be in the form of *what ifs* or turning simple challenges into a never-ending pattern of *it's the end of the world.*

A dance step that often trips up both partners occurs when one partner either believes she/he has the power to read minds (*mind reader*) or can tell the future (*fortune teller*). Many women believe they've been blessed with the gift to read minds; they may even call it a *word of knowledge*. The reality is that they are self-righteous liars. Women cannot read minds, despite their belief they have an intuitive sense. They also cannot predict the future unless the Holy Spirit gives them the gift of prophecy. It's hard to imagine the Holy Spirit giving a wife a prophecy that her husband was going to leave oil stains on the carpet because he forgot to wipe his feet before coming in from the garage.

Often, men help women in their belief they can read minds. Husbands often say to their wives, "You should have known I liked that" or "You could have guessed I didn't want chicken tonight." This provides ammunition for wives' beliefs that they have these special mind-reading and fortune-telling abilities.

The number of strategic dance steps that people use in relationships to fuel a battle is countless. We don't have room in this book to go over all of them, so the few already mentioned will suffice for now. The key to stopping the battle dance is not to learn more damaging and hurtful dance steps, but it is to learn to use *loving and respectful* dance steps.

Love and Respect: Practical Ways to Change the Battle Dance Steps

God-centered heart. The key to the love and respect dance is a God-centered heart. Each partner, at all times, has the partner's best interest at heart in every decision. Often, this means that each partner has to *die to self,* let go of one's own interest for the betterment of the spouse and family. This doesn't mean letting go of dreams and aspirations. It simply means to put the best interest of your spouse above your interest. If both partners are in the love and respect dance, your partner will in return honor your desires and encourage your best interest.

Good intentions. Another important aspect of having a God-centered heart is to believe, truly believe, that your partner has good intentions for you and has your back covered in all situations. This doesn't mean that your partner will never make a mistake in life. It simply means that when bad decisions are made, it isn't because your partner wanted bad things to happen or was ill-willed; your partner made a mistake. Your partner truly desires to learn and grow from the mistake so if at all possible it isn't repeated in the future.

Agape love. Love and respect is an attitude of the heart. An agape heart is filled with love and good intentions for the betterment of others. When both partners have a God-centered heart, both partners don't have to sweat the challenges because together the love and respect dance steps complement each other.

There are many ways to stop the battle dance, to learn ***Loving and Respectful*** dance steps. It takes a committed heart, making changes in self and not "expecting" changes in your partner. You cannot control others, only yourself. When you change yourself, you've created an opportunity for the dynamics within the marital system to change. Once you've made your changes, the marital system will then change in one of three ways. First option, the marital system can break because the other part of the system refuses to change. Second option, you return to your old ways (battle dance, unloving and disrespectful dance steps) because it becomes too difficult to maintain the changes. Third option, the entire marital system changes and uses loving and respectful dance steps consistently.

Either way, when you are obedient to God and show love and respect to your partner, then you will be rewarded. Granted, if your spouse is not willing to make the necessary changes, it may not seem that you are being rewarded. However, anytime we are obedient to God, we are rewarded. It just may not be in the way we expected … a loving husband, a respectful wife. Trusting in God is important; keeping your eyes on God throughout the process results in godly rewards.

GOOD BOOK
PUBLISHING

www.goodbookpublishing.com